The Bible Says What!?

Michael Wiseman

HYPATIA PRESS

Published by Hypatia Press in the United States in 2021

ISBN: 978-1-83919-352-1

www.hypatiapress.org

"Without the shedding of blood there is no forgiveness"
– Hebrews 9:22

"There is no beast like an angry theologian"
– Emperor Julian

"If anyone does not love the lord – a curse be on him"
– 1 Corinthians 16:22

Contents

Intro

The Bible is considered to be the bestselling book of all time. Most Christians refer to it as the good book. Millions of them claim to find guidance and encouragement within its pages. They believe it holds wonderful, life-altering truths. Yet, Christians do not agree on a particular version or translation of this truth. They have the New International Version, New Living Translation, English Standard Version, King James Version, New King James Version, Modern King James Version, Updated King James Version, and many, many more. The Christian truth comes in a variety of flavors. The biblical quotes found throughout the following chapters will come from the New International Version of the Christian Bible, with a few quotes taken from the King James Version due to the strength of its wording.

Why are there so many different translations and variations of the truth? If Yahweh's truth is made to be accessible to everyone, if he truly wanted his truth to be known to the masses he would come down and explain it to us. Clearing up all of the confusion and malice in the process. Why does Yahweh continue to hide in his golden city? Why does the Christian deity refuse to come down and not only authenticate his existence, but explain to us all which version of the Bible is the most accurate? For the same reason Odin and Brahma won't come down and tell us their truths. Because they don't exist. Yahweh is simply a mythological being made up by people who believed in witches and curses. He is the boogeyman that will get you if you don't behave.

A typical Bible study or sermon consists of carefully selected segments of stories or verses that fit whatever message the speaker is attempting to convey. In many instances, they will ignore the ideas or backstories associated with them. In the coming chapters, we are going to look at the parts of the Bible most pastors are afraid to address from their pulpits. We will confront the uncomfortable questions.

A significant contributor to a Christian stepping away from their beliefs is them sitting down and actually reading the book they have been preaching from. I will admit, I was one of those Bible believers that never read the whole book. I went to church three times a week and followed what I was being taught, never looking for myself, never investigating further. Picking up the Bible and reading the stories I had been taught as a kid helped me along my journey. It showed me that my beliefs had been based off someone else's interpretation of the stories, their idea of what the context should be. Reading the Bible was one of the many steps I took along the way. The more people are willing to question their strongly held beliefs the better off humanity will be in the long run.

I, for one, completely endorse Christians reading their Bibles. And for those believers with children, I suggest reading a chapter a night to your kids. From beginning to end. No fair skipping or cutting out parts. It should lead to some exciting bedtime talks.

Most Christians will proclaim their deity, Yahweh, to be loving, all-knowing, all-powerful, and perfect. Using the Bible, they will attempt to validate these claims. The idea that Yahweh is an all-knowing deity comes from 1 John 3:20, which states that "He knows everything." His perfection is referred to in Matthew 5:48, which tells us to be "perfect," just like Yahweh is "perfect." For his loving nature, they will turn to 1 John 4:8, which claims that "God is love," or to the infamous John 3:16, for Yahweh "so loved the world."

As we will see in the preceding chapters, the deity that is described in the Bible is a lot of things, but love, all-knowing, all-powerful, and perfect he is not. Yahweh's own words will condemn him; his contradictions and barbaric concept of morality will shatter any notion of a loving, competent, or just being. For this book, we are going to assume all of the events and ideas described within the Bible, including the deity it represents, are real. We will take the Bible as a literal source of Yahwistic history.

Chapter 1

In the Beginning…

From birth, I was indoctrinated into the ancient monotheistic cult classic, Christianity. My family proudly represents the evangelical, Bible-thumping, hardcore-for-Jesus version of this religion. Plastered on the wall next to the entrance of my parents' home is a giant decal that reads, "As for me and my house, we will serve the Lord. –Joshua 24:15." Following their religion is not a choice; it is a requirement for all who inhabit their home. Both of my parents are ordained ministers and are heavily active in the church. Using the Bible and their own interpretation of its texts, they teach a class in which they instruct others on how to grow in their relationship with Yahweh. My grandparents formed a gospel group, traveling across the country singing old hymns at different churches. They call themselves the End Times Singers. They are extremely excited about an apocalypse they believe will be coming soon. I have three younger siblings who have all followed in my parents' footsteps and found their place within the church as well. With the amount of indoctrination that we were all exposed to, it was inevitable that one, if not all, of us would give in to the unrelenting persistence to follow in their beliefs and worship their deity. We attended church twice on Sundays and once on Wednesday evenings. It was not only the church services I would have to be present for, there was praise and worship practice, of which both my parents had a role in, pot lucks, youth group events, men's meetings, and women's meetings. If the doors to the church were open, we were there.

By taking me to Sunday school, my parents believed that they were saving me from the eternal damnation that their loving deity, Yahweh, had planned for me. It was in Sunday school that I was led to believe in extraordinary things. I was told stories of the Christian deity killing children in their sleep and drowning them for disobedience, narratives I was taught were actual historical events. I was shown accounts of ancient genocides and curses. Validated by the adults around me, my gullible child brain soaked up and believed every word.

With the introduction of an imaginary, fatal condition called sin, they furthered their grip on my naïve mind. I was taught that I was broken, and due to this brokenness, this condition, I was therefore condemned to spend eternity in a lake of fire. I was led to believe that I was born with this condition and that a blood debt was required to save me from my flawed state, to save me from going to hell.

Hell was a place where all of my flesh would be burned off daily and then grown back, just to be scorched off again and again and again for all eternity. Fear was branded into my subconscious. Fear of the hellfire that awaited me if I faltered. Fear of angering a deity that was willing to drown every animal, man, woman, child, and infant on the planet when they failed to follow his commands.

Once the notion of a lethal and damning condition had been established, they presented a cure saturated in the blood of an innocent. I needed to be washed in the blood of an ancient demigod in order to cleanse myself of all my sins and save my eternal soul. There was a catch though, some fine print to go along with this empty cure. If I did not believe that this demigod had died for me and was raised from the dead, if I did not ask him to live inside of me, or if I died with sin in my heart, the Christian deity would send me to his special pit of suffering, without hesitation.

Despite all the threats with eternal anguish, I was told of this deity's overwhelming love for me. He did not care that I was broken;

he loved me anyway, as long as I followed the rules. My parents and grandparents both claimed that Yahweh loved me more than they ever could. My father once told me that the most important thing in the whole world to him was Yahweh, and that his deity came first before anything or anyone, even his children.

Fear is a very powerful weapon. Fear of everlasting pain and suffering. Fear of not being loved because you are broken. The Christian deity had convicted me of my crimes when I was in the womb, and only he could truly love such an imperfect, unworthy person. This was all I knew. It was normal to me. I did not know anything else.

The majority of my earliest childhood church memories take place in a building that had been converted from something resembling an old feed store. This was the first building that housed the church I would attend until the day I left religion. It had a rickety old wooden playset that always gave the kids splinters. The room they called the sanctuary was a vast space, filled with tattered cloth chairs, all facing a stage that was set about four feet off the ground. The stage was covered with a thin blue carpet that was frayed and worn in several places. I can still remember the smell of burnt coffee and donuts that filled the sanctuary every Sunday morning.

The rooms designated for our indoctrination were small and windowless. The unpainted drywall was littered with propaganda posters of a white Jesus interacting with overjoyed children. A large wooden cross stood in the back of the room, draped with a purple cloth and topped with a crown of thorns. Blood was painted into the rivets of the blemished old cross to remind the children of the gory sacrifice that was required to keep them from going to Yahweh's personal palace of affliction.

I was taught hymns celebrating the slaughter of the Christian demigod and how his blood should be desired and sought after. We would happily sing of bathing ourselves in fountains of this holy blood. I performed rituals in which I would take a small cup of watered-down grape juice, hold it up to the ceiling, proclaim it to be the blood of my savior, and drink it. I would drink this ceremonial juice as a reminder of the blood sacrifice that was made by the

Christian demigod in my stead. I would then hold up a cracker and proclaim it to be his flesh, eating it in remembrance of his broken body. As a child, I was taught how to participate in ritualistic pretend cannibalism.

On several occasions, the adult evening service would go longer than our Sunday school, and our teachers, done with their lesson plan, would release us to our parents in the sanctuary. On one of these occasions, I witnessed, for the first time, what Christians call being slain in the spirit or falling under the power of the Christian deity in the form of a ghost. As I entered the sanctuary, I remember seeing many of the adults crying, which was not an uncommon thing to witness. But, as I approached the front of the sanctuary, where my parents typically sat, I saw several people scattered in front of the stage lying on the ground with small blue sheets draped over their waists. Some were rolling around, while others were more still, but all of them were shaking and crying. One of the men started laughing uncontrollably. It was funny at first, and I didn't quite get it, but when I saw one of my mother's friends in front of me, convulsing and crying out for Jesus to save her, it stopped being funny. It scared me. I had never seen an adult act this way before. They seemed to be in various degrees of anguish, distress, and madness. The music coming from the stage seemed to entrance them. The mellow rhythmic sounds of the guitar, keyboard, and drums were hypnotic. The man with the guitar was repeating slowly and emphatically into the microphone, "Thank you, Jesus. Thank you, Jesus. Thank you, Jesus."

As time passed, each adult gradually came to, wiped away their tears and smeared makeup, and went about their lives as if nothing had happened. I watched this phenomenon go on for years. Many would claim to have received spiritual direction or healing. Some thought that Yahweh was giving them prophetic words and predictions. I witnessed my own parents falling to the ground under the power of Yahweh's ghost. Undergoing the minimal possession of this spirit, they never shouted or laughed or caused a scene. Sometimes they would cry, not sob or cry out though. Usually, they would just lie there with their eyes closed, resting peacefully. It was more intimate for them; they thought they were communing with their creator deity through some kind of psychic link with his detached spirit.

When I was about twelve years old, my mother pushed for me to get prayed over by the pastor during an altar call to receive what he called the "power of the Holy Spirit." I eventually gave in to the pressure, reluctantly walked up to the front of the sanctuary, and stood in line. Waiting for my turn, I watched as, one by one, the adults in front of me walked up to the pastor and fell to the ground. I began to get nervous when the man in front of me stepped forward; I was next. The pastor touched the man's forehead with his thumb, and the man began to sway. The pastor prayed loudly and forcefully. The man began to sway again, but this time he fell straight back into the arms of the waiting ushers. The ushers laid him down gently and placed a little blue blanket over his waist and walked toward me as I stepped forward. They took their place behind me and waited for the whole process to start again. The pastor's hands were clasped in front of him and his head was raised toward the sky. Mumbling "Amen" and "Praise Jesus" repeatedly under his breath, he lowered his head and focused his attention on me. His liver-spotted hands reached out and grabbed mine, squeezing them firmly. He drew his face close and told me that Yahweh had big plans for me. He told me that I was going to be a youth pastor and bring thousands of souls to Jesus. The pastor reached into his pocket, pulled out a small bottle of oil, dabbed some on his thumb, and pressed it to my forehead.

I could smell the stale coffee on his breath as he prayed and spouted out words I did not understand. He began to press harder against my forehead with his oily thumb. I resisted, which only made him shout louder and push harder. After a while, he realized that I was not going to succumb to his holy apparition. So with an "Amen" and a pat on the shoulder, he released me unto the congregation. As far as the Holy Spirit is concerned, I have never experienced anything beyond that feeling you get when you sing along with one of your favorite songs on the radio. The Holy Ghost is nothing more than adrenaline and goose-bumps wrongly categorized as supernatural occurrences or interventions. After numerous failed attempts by many different pastors at various youth ministries and camps, I was never slain in the spirit; I never fell over.

Church camp was a time for kids to socialize with a bunch of other kids from other churches. The majority of my memories from camp are good ones. But it was at the nightly church services when things would change from fun and games to turn or burn. We would all gather in a large auditorium. The pastors would preach of our sinful nature. They told us we all deserved eternal hellfire because of this. They broke us down. They made us feel inferior, unworthy, flawed, and helpless. We were told we were filthy and vile to Yahweh.

Once brought down to the lowest form of scum we were told to ask Yahweh to forgive us for being this way. They wanted me to bow down and praise him for his willingness to care about and save a wretch like me. Once we begged for mercy, they wanted us to be bathed in the blood of a demigod to become pure and holy. To be accepted.

The words took their toll. Kids wept and fell to their knees. Cries for a savior, to be loved, to be freed from bondage or worldly influence rang out while the praise and worship team would play soft entrancing melodies. Kids formed small groups to cry with each other and speak for Yahweh. Mission accomplished. Our emotions had been played like a well-tuned piano. Once reduced to our worthless state, these preachers, these religious zealots had to keep at it. We needed to be reminded, to be re-broken. Again and again and again.

I was taught to never deny my belief. I was told stories of Christians being lined up and ordered to deny their faith or be shot. When they all refused, they were slaughtered. I was to be like them. I was taught that those who deny Yahweh to save their own skin are considered "lukewarm" Christians, and Yahweh would "spit" them "out" (Revelation 3:16). They told us that there might come a time when we would have to make that very choice. And if I made the wrong choice, Jesus would act as if he "never knew" me (Matthew 7:23). I was also taught to believe that this life was only temporary and if I denied Yahweh before death, I would be "thrown into the lake of fire" (Revelation 20:15). To me as a small child, the threats were made real by the adults advocating for their validity.

The indoctrination in my life was constant. Day in and day out. You're not worthy unless you're bathed in the blood. You are nothing without Jesus. If you're not a strong enough Christian Yahweh will spit you out, like he never knew you. Jesus is coming soon, you better be prepared. Turn or burn.

My parents felt it best to shelter me from anything that did not fit into their Jesus bubble. The less outside worldly influence I was exposed to, the less likely I was to conform to the ways of the world and burn in hell for all eternity. The only kind of music I was allowed to listen to was Christian music, and even then, my father had to verify that the bands only honored Jesus with their lyrics. Listening to oldies on the radio was prohibited. One time my father heard an oldies song that talked about kissing a girl in the backseat of a car, therefore all music that did not glorify Yahweh was wicked and forbidden. Movies rated as low as PG had to be viewed first to make sure they were appropriate. If they said "Jesus" or "Christ" as a curse word, then they were using Yahweh's name in vain and we were forbidden to watch it. Cartoons with any kind of magic, witches, spells, or goblins were the work of the devil and only there to lure children to hell. Even the food I ate had to be free from demonic influence; deviled eggs became angel eggs, and devil's food cake was just never eaten. I was shrouded from reality, kept in the dark about how the world works for fear of my immortal soul.

Indoctrination did not stop at home or at church. My entire schooling took place at different Christian institutions where Bible classes were part of the daily curriculum, and on Thursday's, we had mandatory chapel. Every morning, in every classroom, every child would pledge allegiance to our country's flag and then to the Christian flag:

"I pledge allegiance to the Christian Flag and to the savior for whose Kingdom it stands. One Savior, crucified, risen, and coming again with life and liberty to all who believe. Amen."

After swearing our loyalty to our religion, via the Christian flag, we pledged our allegiance to the Bible as well:

"I pledge allegiance to the Bible, God's Holy Word. I will make it a lamp unto my feet and a light unto my path and will hide its words in my heart that I might not sin against God. Amen."

Once a week, in first grade, my teacher would ask the class to sit down and form a large circle. She would then put a flashlight in the middle of the circle of children and turn off all the lights. She asked us all to close our eyes and wait for the Holy Spirit to talk to us. We were trying to summon a ghost to possess our thoughts and speak through us. Whenever we performed this ritual, there was this one kid who never failed to receive special instructions from Yahweh. He was consistently being told by the Christian deity to sit next to his friend. It showed me at an early age how some people could manipulate and lie about their interactions with Yahweh to get what they want out of life. The kid with the message from Yahweh always got what he wanted; he always got to sit next to his friend.

After junior high, I was put into a home school program called the A.C.E. program. A.C.E. stands for "accelerated Christian education." To say the schooling I received was insufficient for the educational purposes of a high school student is a massive understatement. I was learning how to properly address an envelope in the ninth grade. My history books had crosses and Bible verses depicted on them. The diploma I received upon graduation contained Proverbs 1:7:

"The fear of the Lord is the beginning of knowledge."

The indoctrination ran deep.

As I grew into my teens, I struggled with my beliefs. I constantly felt my faith dwindling away, and yet in the back of my mind, a fear lingered, the fear of having my flesh burned off every day for eternity.

My mind was plagued by it. I feared the eternal consequences of every action I took.

Eventually, as an adult, I put away my childish fears and filled my mind with more productive things, like movie quotes and song lyrics. Years later, I was out with a friend and we happened upon a Christian radio show that was doing a live reading of the Bible from beginning to end on the steps of city hall. There were at least twenty peppy Christian college kids passing out tracts and interacting with people. I knew there were issues with the religion and I knew there were issues within the Bible itself, but I froze. I could not think of a single rebuttal to anything they presented to me. I was completely unprepared. This would not happen again.

That failure had a profound effect on me. I went back to my Bible and started reading it from the beginning. I wrote out the ridiculous narratives and concepts that I found inside Yahweh's bestseller. I found so many issues they could no longer be contained within the notebooks and note cards that littered my office. I had to put it all in a book.

As the book began to take shape, my yearning to ask Christians some of the questions that came up when reading the Bible grew. I could no longer stay silent. One day, on the way home from work, I called the number on one of those Bible billboards scattered throughout the United States. I had a great hour-long conversation with the man who picked up the phone. I began contacting my new friend whenever I would think of a new question. Eventually, he grew tired of my examination into his beliefs and blocked me. I was cut off.

With my billboard friend gone, I resorted to online engagements with believers. This format quickly proved to be slow and frustrating, so I called a church and asked to speak to a pastor. Everything changed when that first pastor came on the line and failed to come up with answers to simple questions. I knew I had to call more pastors, and I knew someone out there would want to hear those conversations. So I created a podcast called "The Bible Says What!?" On the show, I talk with religious leaders from all over the world and discuss their beliefs and why they believe them. With the podcast, I found the outlet I needed to confront those who adhere to the constraints of a religious belief. Those with influence, not just pastors, but authors, podcasters, and theologians. Those looking to spread their particular version of Christianity to others.

The result has been a rollercoaster of guests and encounters. My questions and blunt approach do not sit well with everyone. I have received threats with civil suits and been hung up on quite a few times. Regardless, I love the conversation, the back and forth, the rebuttals, and the silence after a tough question; I love podcasting. Through it all, I have learned a great deal about myself and the craft I reluctantly picked up.

I know first-hand that conversations like these change lives. I will admit, I was one of those Bible believers who never read the whole book. I went to church and followed what I was being taught, never looking for myself, never investigating further. These types of conversations and books have helped me along my journey, and my hope is that my conversations and this book will be beneficial the way so many others have been for me. The more people who are willing to question their strongly held beliefs, the better off humanity will be in the long run.

Atheists who actively engage with Christians are often asked why we waste so much time and effort on a belief that we do not find to be true? Why can we not let people just believe whatever it is they want to believe and leave them alone? Most outspoken atheists will get at least one of these questions at some point. Each atheist will have their own, oftentimes personal, reasons for opposing or confronting religion, whether they were subjected to it at some point in their life or know someone else that has been. Some of us argue against religious ideology so that people can make better more informed decisions at home and at the ballot box. I do it for my children. I do it for your children and their future. I want them all to grow up in a world free from the detrimental grip religion has on our society—a world where ignorance is an endangered species on its way to becoming extinct. I do it because the Bible wielded in the hands of monsters will always be used as a weapon. Let's start the book.

Chapter 2

The Inconsistent Truth

Every story, every parable, every "prophecy of Scripture" found within the Bible, did not come from man, but was "spoke from" Yahweh and written down by humans that were influenced "by the Holy Spirit" (2 Peter 1:20-21). Man may have penned the Bible, but Yahweh claims to have given him the words to put in it. The Bible says that "all Scripture" has been "breathed" out by Yahweh and is "useful for teaching, rebuking, correcting and training in righteousness" (2 Tim. 3:16). The Christian holy book, the Bible in its totality, is a book that contains the spoken words of the Christian deity, and his every word, according to himself, "is flawless" (2 Samuel 22:31). If Yahweh is truly not the author of "disorder" and believes his entire book to be a reliable source for an abundance of theocratic purposes, then we should find nothing inside that is confusing or contradictory (1 Corinthians 14:33). Nevertheless, throughout our journey, we will encounter many contradicting narratives and ideas.

The first biblical inconstancy we are going to look at comes from within the very first two chapters of Yahweh's bestseller. In chapter one of Genesis, Yahweh tells us that after making all of the animals, he "created mankind," both "male and female" (Genesis 1:27). The creation sequence in chapter one starts with animals and ends with man and woman being created together. Yet in the very next chapter of Genesis, the Christian deity claims to have created the man first, then all of the animals, and then the "woman from the rib" of that man (Genesis 2:22).

Who came first: Adam or the chicken? We will never know because Yahweh gives us two different timelines for his creation story. Why would a perfect being author a story in which he contradicts himself? How can a flawless book have two conflicting records of the same event?

In this alternate version of the creation story, the man was created to "work the ground" (Genesis 2:5). Yahweh placed him "in the Garden of Eden" to "take care of it" (Genesis 2:15). Being a large garden, he decided the man would need a "helper" (Genesis 2:18). So, Yahweh "formed…the wild animals and all the birds in the sky" and "livestock" to provide him assistance (Genesis 2:19-20). On his first try, Yahweh failed to find his man a "suitable helper" (Genesis 2:20). His next idea however, was a bit more successful. He decided to create "woman," completing his breeding pair of humans (Genesis 2:22). How does an all-knowing being fail to get something right the first time?

As we look deeper into the creation story, it develops other problematic differences. Did Yahweh create "every winged bird" out "of the sea" (Genesis 1:20-21)? Or, did "all the birds in the sky" emerge from "the ground" (Genesis 2:19)? Did Yahweh take all of the "water" that was pre-existing "under the sky" to form the oceans, separating them from the "dry ground" (Genesis 1:9)? Or did he require the water to come "up from the earth and" flood "the whole surface of the ground" (Genesis 2:6)? These small conflicting details were supposed to have been arranged by a perfect deity.

The stories that record the birth, life, death, and resurrection of the Christian demigod, are, to the majority of Christians, among the most important stories found within the Bible. And yet every one of the books that contain these events contradicts each other at one point or another.

Matthew and Luke are the only two books of the Bible that document the birth of the Christian demigod. According to the book of Luke, "Mary," the mother-to-be of "Jesus," was visited by an "angel" who informed her that she was going to have a "son" (Luke 1:30-31). This "angel" explained to Mary that one day "the Holy Spirit will come" to her "and the power of the Most High will overshadow" and impregnate her (Luke 1:35).

In the book of Matthew, it was "Joseph," the future stepfather of Jesus, who received a visit from "an angel" (Matthew 1:20). Joseph's angel notified him that his wife-to-be would "give birth to a son," and that he would not be the father of this child (Matthew 1:21). The baby "conceived in her" womb would come "from the Holy Spirit," from Yahweh himself (Matthew 1:20). The angel was clear, Joseph had no connection to Jesus genetically. The Bible implies that Jesus was a bastard child born out of supernatural insemination.

Most Christians claim that Jesus was from the bloodline of King David, the famous Old Testament Bible hero who slayed the giant "Philistine" using only "a sling and a stone" (1 Samuel 17:50). They believe this was foretold in the Old Testament. The verses used to confirm this idea not only fail to mention that Jesus would be coming from the lineage of David, but they also stand in contradiction to one another. The proof brought forth by Christians brings further discrepancies to light.

In 2 Samuel, Yahweh promises to "establish the throne of" David's "kingdom forever" (2 Samuel 7:12-13). Unlike his affections for the previous king, "Saul," when the line of David "does wrong" Yahweh "will punish him with a rod wielded by men," but his "love will never be taken away from him" (2 Samuel 7:14-15). Yahweh does not assign any terms and conditions to this promise. He clearly states that David's line will "endure," and be loved no matter what they do, "forever" (2 Samuel 7:16). In the book of Psalm, Yahweh claims that he will "establish" David's "throne" for "as long as the heavens endure" (Psalm 89:29). Even "if they violate" his "decrees and fail to keep" his "commands," Yahweh promises he "will not violate" the "covenant or alter" the deal in any way (Psalm 89:31-34).

14

Other verses used to promote the idea that Jesus will be of David's lineage come from 2 Chronicles and 1 Kings. In both of these books, Yahweh adds some fine print to his covenant with David. If David's descendants "do all" Yahweh commands (2 Chronicles 7:17), "and observe" all of his "decrees and laws" (1 Kings 9:4-6), then he will honor his promise to David. Yahweh either forgot that he promised to honor his "covenant" even "if they violate" his "decrees" and "fail to keep" his "commands," or he decided to break his previously sworn agreement and add some stipulations to it (Psalm 89:31-34).

Christians will see what they want to see. They will interpret or alter the Bible to fit their narrative, or their idea of what the narrative should be. These verses never state that Jesus will be coming from the lineage of David. Christians use the Bible as a giant connect-the-dots with no numbers or clear outcome. They have to create connections that are not there. They will throw in lines connecting verses and events to fit their own wishful thinking.

In Matthew 1 and Luke 3, we find a genealogy connecting Jesus to David that implies Jesus came from the lineage of Joseph rather than Mary. According to Matthew, the lineage of "Joseph, the husband of Mary," leads back to David (Matthew 1:16). And the book of Luke states that "Jesus…was thought" to be "the son of Joseph," and then proceeds to give a genealogy for Joseph's side of the family connecting him to David (Luke 3:23). If Mary was supernaturally inseminated, and Joseph clearly had no biological connection to Jesus, why not use Mary's family tree? Why force a connection to David through someone who was not even a blood relative?

Things only get more obscure when we look into the books that contain the birth of the Christian demigod. According to the birth account found in the book of Matthew, the evil "King Herod" had become "disturbed" upon receiving news from a group of "Magi" regarding the birth of the one they called the "king of the Jews" (Matthew 2:1-3). Magi is the plural form of magus, which is defined by dictionary.com as a sorcerer or a person who possesses magical powers. The Bible says that these magical people told "King Herod" they were following a star and that this "star" was leading them to a child, who was to be the "king of the Jews" (Matthew 2:1-2). Jealous of this child's self-proclaimed royal status, the evil King Herod "sent" the magical people "to Bethlehem" so they could "report to" him the child's location (Matthew 2:8).

The Magi eventually found the baby Jesus hiding out in a "house" (Matthew 2:11). They "presented him with gifts of gold, frankincense and myrrh" (Matthew 2:11). They gave their gifts to the infant king and left. They chose "not to go back to Herod," and report the location of the child as he had asked (Matthew 2:12). But the baby Jesus was still not safe from the evil King.

Later that night, while "Joseph" was asleep, "an angel" revealed to him "in a dream" that King "Herod" was searching "for the child to kill him" (Matthew 2:13). Joseph heeded the angelic warning and "took the child and his" wife-to-be "during the night and left for Egypt" (Matthew 2:14). The birth of Jesus, as described in the book of Matthew, contains escapes from a mad King and a bright star leading an unknown number of magical people to the birthplace of a child, they called the king of the Jews. The book of Luke records the events of Jesus' birth, completely different.

According to the book of Luke, there was no danger from a king named Herod, no bright star, and no magical people with presents. The birth scene of the baby Jesus in Luke takes place in the same city as Matthew, Bethlehem. Unlike Matthew, which claims the Magi found baby Jesus in a "house" (Matthew 2:11), Luke says that "Mary" gave birth to Jesus "and placed him in a manger, because there was no guest room available for them" at the inn where they had stopped (Luke 2:7). No house is ever mentioned.

According to Luke, Yahweh sent an "angel" down to bring "the good news" of "great joy" of his son's birth to a small group of "shepherds" that were "living out in the fields nearby" Bethlehem (Luke 2:8-10). The angel told them that a "Savior" had been born in the city and that they should go and check it out (Luke 2:11-12). Why would Yahweh only inform a few shepherds in one field? Why not send hordes of angels to the whole city or the whole world proclaiming this good news?

Feeling the attention drift away from himself, Yahweh sent down "a great company of the heavenly hosts" to start "praising" him and giving him all the "glory" (Luke 2:13-14). Why did Yahweh send only one angel to announce the great news of his son's birth, but then send down a large group of angels to praise and glorify himself? Why is the Christian deity so self-centered?

In the book of Luke, the baby Jesus does not get chased from Bethlehem by an evil king, as stated in the book of Matthew. Instead, with time to relax, "Mary" sat up and "pondered" the events that had taken place that evening (Luke 2:19). Both of these stories cannot be accurate. Christians have to either ignore the blatant contradictions or make excuses for them.

In the book of Kings, we find a man named Elijah, who possessed special abilities given to him by Yahweh; he was one of the Christian deity's most powerful employees. He was so powerful that he once raised a child from the dead by stretching "himself out on the boy three times" (1 Kings 17:21). One day our new Bible buddy Elijah was walking with a friend along the river. When "suddenly a chariot of fire" appeared in front of them (2 Kings 2:11). Elijah was swept up by Yahweh's enchanted flaming carriage and "went up to heaven in a whirlwind" (2 Kings 2:11). Elijah ascended into heaven, never to walk the earth again.

The contradiction occurs when Jesus claims in the book of John that "no one has ever gone into heaven except...the Son of Man," Jesus himself (John 3:13). Did the Christian demigod not read 2 Kings? Has Elijah not been up in heaven hanging out with Yahweh since his ascension in the Old Testament? How does Jesus, the earthly extension of the Christian deity, the deity that asserts to know everything, not know about Elijah's ascension into heaven?

Jesus also made the claim that "no one has seen" the Christian deity (John 6:46). According to Jesus himself, the one who should have first-hand knowledge of who Yahweh has seen, tells us "no one has ever seen" Yahweh (John 1:18). Furthermore, the book of

1Timothy says "no one has seen or can see" the Christian deity (1 Timothy 6:16). As it turns out, the Bible recorded several people seeing the Christian deity.

Adam and Eve are the first people in the Bible documented as having observed the Christian deity in person. Ashamed of their nakedness, they "heard the sound of" Yahweh "walking in the garden," so "they hid from" him (Genesis 3:8). The Christian deity finds them hiding "among the trees" and then curses them for eating forbidden things (Genesis 3:8). Adam and Eve heard the physical footsteps of the Christian deity; Yahweh was present in the garden. He even had a harsh talk with them after he found them hiding in the trees. The Bible implies that Adam and Eve stood in the presence of the Christian deity contradicting the idea in the book of John that no one has ever seen him.

Furthermore, the Bible says that Moses sat and had a conversation with Yahweh "face to face, as one speaks to a friend" (Exodus 33:11). When the Christian deity talks to his friend Moses he does so "face to face," meaning Moses was looking right at Yahweh (Numbers 12:8). In the book of Exodus, Yahweh tells us that "Moses" took his brother "Aaron," a couple of guys named "Nadab and Abihu, and…seventy elders of Israel," up to the mountain of Yahweh, where they all "saw the God of Israel" (Exodus 24: 9-10). Yahweh makes it very clear that "they saw" him up on his mountain (Exodus 24:11). Isaiah saw Yahweh with his own "eyes" (Isaiah 6:5). Even the biblical character "Jacob…saw" the Christian deity "face to face" (Genesis 32:30). According to Yahweh's own breathed out words, no one has ever seen him, and yet he tells us that many have stood in his presence and seen him. Why would Yahweh contradict his own words? Why would he not tell the truth about something so trivial?

The Bible says that near the end of his life, the Christian demigod visited the city of Jerusalem. This event is documented in four books of the Bible: Matthew, Mark, Luke, and John. The book of Mark, the earliest source we have out of the four, claims that as Jesus "approached Jerusalem," he asked his disciples to "go to the village ahead of" them, where they would "find a colt tied" up (Mark 11:1-2). Jesus refused to go into the city on foot, and for reasons untold to us, he was unwilling to retrieve the colt on his own. He needed his disciples to go "untie it" and "bring it" to him (Mark 11:2). When his disciples returned with the borrowed colt, they "threw their cloaks over it," and Jesus "sat on it" (Mark 11:7). The Christian demigod made his grand entrance into the city on top of the colt, and "many people spread their cloaks" and "branches they had cut in the fields" over "the road" as Jesus passed by (Mark 11:8).

This same story is described slightly different in the book of Luke. Jesus tells his disciples to go into a "village" and deliver to him the "colt" they will find "tied" up there (Luke 19:30). His disciples retrieved the colt, "threw their cloaks" onto it, and "put Jesus on it" (Luke 19:35). In Luke's narrative, we are also told the people only "spread their cloaks on the road" when Jesus entered the city; they did not throw any branches down as described in the book of Mark (Luke 19:36).

The book of John adds further confusion to the story. In the book of John, Jesus found "a young donkey" on his own without the help of his disciples (John 12:14). According to this variation of the same account, when the Christian demigod rode into Jerusalem, no one threw their cloaks out on the road. "Palm branches" were the only thing they brought with them to throw (John 12:13).

The last book describing this event, Matthew, contains the most ridiculous version of this story. Similar to the books of Mark and Luke, the Matthew account begins with Jesus telling his disciples to "go to the village ahead of" them where they will "find a donkey tied" up (Matthew 21:2). The donkey in the book of Matthew was an adult and not alone; she had a "colt by her" (Matthew 21:2). Again, we are told that Jesus is unable to retrieve the animal by himself and assigns the job to his disciples, who obediently "untie them" both "and bring them to" him (Matthew 21:2). The disciples "brought the donkey and the colt" to Jesus, so he could "sit on" them (Matthew 21:7). While the people watched this absurd spectacle, they "spread their cloaks" and "cut branches from the trees and

19

spread them on the road" just as they did in the book of Mark (Matthew 21:8). There are so many variations of the same story. How can Yahweh be seen as a credible source of truth if he twists the details of the stories he records?

Additional problematic differences are found in the story of the crucifixion of Jesus. The four books of the Bible that contain this story, Matthew, Mark, Luke, and John, all agree that the Christian demigod was crucified alongside two others. Yet they do not all agree on the details of this event. The book of John, briefly mentions "two others" who were "crucified" with Jesus, "one on each side" of him (John 19:18). The book of John merely states that these others were there and then never brings them up again. The book of Matthew describes these others as "two rebels" that "heaped insults" onto the dying Christian demigod (Matthew 27:44). The book of Mark validates the Matthew account, stating that the "two rebels" who were crucified with Jesus "heaped insults on him" (Mark 15:32). The book of Luke, however, simply refers to the "two other men" as "criminals" without naming a crime and then completely contradicts all the other narratives (Luke 23:32). According to the book of Luke, "one of the criminals who hung there" next to the Christian demigod "hurled insults at him" while the other criminal asked him to "remember" him when he got to heaven (Luke 23:39-42). Did both criminals hurl insults at the Christian demigod, or was it just one of them? We will never know because Yahweh could not get his stories straight.

What were the last words spoken by the Christian demigod? What did he cry out before he took his last breath, and what happened after he died? Again, Matthew, Mark, Luke, and John all cover this event, although they do not all agree on the details. The book of Matthew and the book of Mark both claim that Jesus yelled out, "My God, my God, why have you forsaken me?" just before he died (Matthew 27:46) (Mark 15:34). They also agree that as Jesus died, the "curtain" that was in the "temple" tore from "top to bottom" (Matthew 27:51) (Mark 15:38). However, according to only Matthew, when Jesus died, the "earth shook, the rocks split," breaking open the "tombs" of "many holy people" (Matthew 27:51-52). The book of Matthew goes on to tell us that the corpses of these holy people were "raised to life," and that they walked around the city and "appeared to many people" (Matthew 27:52-53).

The book of Luke contradicts the accounts given to us in Matthew and Mark. Luke claims Jesus said, "Father, into your hands I commit my spirit," and then died (Luke 23:46). Based on this timeline, Jesus told his dad that he was ready to die and did so without any extraordinary events taking place.

Further diluting the truth, the book of John asserts that the last words of Jesus before he died, were "it is finished" (John 19:30). No earthquakes took place in the book of John. No undead holy people walked around in the book of Luke. How are we to know which one is telling the truth? Which book contains the correct account?

For most Christians, the resurrection of the Christian demigod is one of the most significant events in the Bible. If Jesus had not come back to life, then all of their "preaching is useless and so is" their "faith" (1 Corinthians 15:14). Given the immense importance of the resurrection account, one might assume that Yahweh would want his followers to know exactly how the events of the day unfolded—he would want them to know the truth.

What we find instead is yet another collection of conflicting details and storylines. The Bible says in 1 Corinthians that after Jesus was resurrected "on the third day," he appeared to Peter first and then to the twelve disciples (1 Corinthians 15:4). "After that," we are told, "he appeared to more than five hundred of" his followers "at the same time" (1 Corinthians 15:6). Once he had shown himself to hundreds of people, Jesus "appeared to James, then to all the apostles, and last of all, he appeared to" Paul (1 Corinthians 15:7-8).

The book of Matthew recounts a different sequence of events. According to the timeline in the book of Matthew, "after the Sabbath," when "Mary Magdalene and the other Mary" arrived "at the tomb" where the body of Jesus was being kept, "a violent earthquake" occurred and "an angel," whose "appearance was like lightning," descended "from heaven" (Matthew 28:1-3). The angel "rolled back the stone" that was covering the entrance to the tomb and then "sat on it" (Matthew 28:2). This singular angel informed both of the Marys that Jesus was no longer there; he had been "risen, just as he said" he would be (Matthew 28:6).

The angelic being revealed the empty tomb and told the women to "go quickly and tell his disciples" that Jesus had "risen from the dead and" that he was going to meet them in "Galilee," where they would be able to "see him" (Matthew 28:7). Ecstatic, the two women hurried to tell the disciples about what they had seen and heard. Before they could reach their destination, "Jesus" showed up alive and well, appearing to both Marys first (Matthew 28:9), completely contradicting the timeline of events told to us in 1 Corinthians 15:5-8. The women immediately ran to him, "clasped his feet and worshiped him" (Matthew 28:9). Repeating the angel's message, Jesus told the women to let his disciples know that he would meet them in "Galilee" (Matthew 28:10).

Eventually, Jesus revealed himself to "eleven" of his "disciples" in "Galilee" (Matthew 28:16). There were only eleven disciples at this time, and not the inaccurately stated twelve as in 1 Corinthians 15:5. At this point in the story, Judas, the disciple who betrayed Jesus, was dead. How did this obvious blunder get put into Yahweh's perfect book?

Contradicting the previous claims in Matthew and 1 Corinthians, Yahweh tells us an entirely different version of the resurrection story in the book of Mark. The book of Mark claims that after the Sabbath "Mary Magdalene, Mary the mother of James, and" a woman whom Yahweh neglected to mention in the previous versions of this story named "Salome," all went to the tomb where the body of Jesus was being kept (Mark 16:1). When they arrived at the tomb, they saw that "the stone" that blocked the entrance "had been rolled away" (Mark 16:4). "As they entered the tomb, they saw a young man dressed in a white robe sitting" inside (Mark 16:5). The young man in white told the women that "Jesus the Nazarene, who was crucified" was no longer in the tomb because he had been "risen" from the dead (Mark 16:6). He needed the women to get a message to the disciples that Jesus was alive and wanted to meet them in "Galilee" (Mark 16:7). Unfortunately, the women were so terrified by the young man that they "went out and fled from the tomb" and did not inform the disciples about what they saw or heard (Mark 16:8). That is where the book of Mark ends according to our oldest sources of this document.

However, the extended version of Mark claims that "Jesus rose early on the first day of the week" and again "appeared first to Mary Magdalene" (Mark 16:9). This time Mary did not flee in terror, "she went and told" the disciples about her encounter with Jesus (Mark 16:10). Why did Jesus need messengers? Why use a young boy and Mary to spread the news of his resurrection? Was he not capable of telling the disciples himself?

"Later Jesus appeared to the Eleven as they were eating" one evening (Mark 16:14). During his visit, the Christian demigod prophesied that "those who believe" will be able "pick up snakes," heal "sick people," and if "they drink deadly poison, it will not hurt them at all" (Mark 16:17-18). The Bible teaches us that as long as you do these foolish acts in the "name" of Yahweh and "believe" that Jesus rose from the dead, you will be just fine (Mark 16:17). Later that evening, Jesus "was taken up into heaven," thus concluding the alternate ending given to us in the book of Mark (Mark 16:19).

How many countless followers of Jesus have fallen victim to the Bible's claim that they can drink deadly poison and survive? What about the snake-handling preachers who decided to forgo the poison drinking and take up venomous snake handling? These misguided pastors assume that Mark 16:18 meant deadly serpents. They have to change the sentence in Mark; they have to take the word "deadly" from the drinking poison portion and add it to the snake part of it. Not one place in the Bible does it say that it is a good idea to hold onto deadly serpents while preaching, singing, or dancing. The Christian deity knew what this verse was capable of, he knew the fatal consequences that these words would have, and still, he either put it in himself or allowed it into his book.

The book of Luke describes these events a bit differently. According to the timeline in Luke, "Mary Magdalene, Joanna, Mary the mother of James, and the" unnamed "others with them," all journeyed to the tomb with prepared spices for the body of Jesus (Luke 24:10). The book of Luke expands the guest list to an unknown number of visitors. Who are these extra people, and why do the other books not mention them?

When the group arrived at the tomb, "they found the stone rolled away" with nobody inside (Luke 24:2). "Suddenly two men" appeared wearing "clothes that gleamed like lightning" (24:4). The men told the group that Jesus was no longer there because he had been "risen" from the dead (Luke 24:6). When the group returned from the tomb, "they told" the "Eleven" remaining disciples about everything they had seen and heard (Luke 24:9). The disciples "did not believe the women" (Luke 24:11). "Peter" went down to see for himself and found the body of Jesus missing (Luke 24:12).

Later that day, Jesus walked up to "two" of his disciples and "kept" them "from recognizing him" (Luke 24:13-16). They walked and talked until they "approached the village" they were headed toward (Luke 24:28). By this time, it was getting dark. The disciples "urged him" to "stay with" them for the night (Luke 24:29). Jesus, still not revealing his identity, decided to go "with them" (Luke 24:29).

During dinner that evening, Jesus "broke" the "bread" and "began" handing it out "to them" (Luke 24:30). As he did this, the disciples' "eyes were opened and they recognized him" (Luke 24:31). As soon as they were allowed to see their new friend for who he really was, Jesus "disappeared from their sight" (Luke 24:31).

What was the purpose of hiding his true identity, and then upon revealing it, vanishing into thin air? Why play tricks on people? Why not appear to the whole world and state your name and purpose? Why keep things so hidden?

When the two disciples returned, they told their friends all about their encounter with Jesus. While they were explaining what happened, Jesus appeared and "stood among them" (Luke 24:36).

24

They were "frightened, thinking they" were seeing "a ghost" (Luke 24:37). Jesus tried to calm the disciples, reminding them that ghosts do "not have flesh and bones" (Luke 24:39). He invited them to "touch" his body and see for themselves (Luke 24:39). They "still did not believe" his words (Luke 24:41). Amused by their disbelief, Jesus "took" some "fish" and "ate it in" front of them, proving once and for all that he was not a ghost, but the living dead (Luke 24:42-43). After an unknown amount of time passed, the disciples walked their zombified savior out of town, and he "was taken up into heaven" (Luke 24:51).

According to the last book that describes this event, the book of John, "Mary Magdalene went to the tomb" alone (John 20:1). When Mary, who was by herself, "saw that the stone had been removed from the entrance" of the tomb, she ran to get "Simon Peter and the other disciple, the one Jesus loved" (John 20:1-2). Once Peter and the beloved disciple saw that the tomb was empty, they "went back to" their homes, but "Mary stood outside the tomb crying" (John 20:10-11). Mary walked to the entrance and "bent over to look into the tomb and saw two angels in white, seated where Jesus' body had been" (John 20:11-12). When "she turned around" to run, she "saw Jesus standing there, but she did not" recognize him (John 20:14). She thought "he was the gardener" (John 20:15). "Jesus" called Mary's name and immediately she knew who he was (John 20:16).

Later, Jesus appeared to "the disciples" in a "locked" room (John 20:19). When he showed them the wounds on "his hands and side," they "were overjoyed" (John 20:20). Jesus had come to give them a gift. The gift of the Holy Ghost. "Jesus said, 'Peace be with you!'" and then "breathed on them," possessing the disciples with Yahweh's "Holy Spirit" (John 20:21-22). With this apparition equipped, they now had the power to magically "forgive anyone" of their "sins" (John 20:23).

"A week later," Jesus returned to the same "locked" room (John 20:26). The purpose of this visit was to prove to "Thomas," who "was not with the disciples" during Jesus' first visit, that he was alive and well (John 20:24). Thomas saw him and "believed" (John 20:29).

Afterward, Jesus decided he would hang around for a while. According to the book of John, living-dead Jesus and his disciples did a lot together that was "not recorded" in the Bible (John 20:30). Apparently, "the whole world" does "not have room for the books that would be" needed to contain these untold adventures (John 21:25).

Who did Jesus appear to first? Was it Mary or Peter? Did hundreds of people see the risen demigod or just a few? Were there one or two angels at the tomb, or was it a young man? We are unable to know these things because the Bible gives us a multitude of contradicting accounts for the same event. Why did Yahweh produce, or allow to be produced, five opposing narratives? Why does the Bible not give us a clear and accurate description? How are we supposed to know which book got it right?

The final contradiction we are going to cover in this chapter comes from two remarkably similar stories in which the antagonist, the villain of the story, is the contradicting ingredient. In 1 Chronicles 21, the Bible says that "Satan rose up against Israel and incited David," one of the most important biblical kings, "to take a census" of his fighting forces (1 Chronicles 21:1). Satan convinced David to take this headcount, and for reasons we are not given, Yahweh saw this as an "evil" act (1 Chronicles 21:7). After receiving his instructions from Satan, David ordered the "commanders of the troops" to take a headcount of "the Israelites" (1 Chronicles 21:2). This angered the Christian deity. For taking this forbidden census, Yahweh gave David "three options," three different punishments for Yahweh to "carry out against" the Israelites (1 Chronicles 21:10). David was forced to choose either "three years of famine, three months of being swept away before" his "enemies," or "three days...of plague in the land" (1 Chronicles 21:12). David selected option number three, he chose to have the people of Israel stricken by a plague for three days, for a sin none of them committed. Yahweh demanded punishment; he needed lots of innocent people to suffer for David's offensive headcount. The loving Christian deity "sent a plague" that killed "seventy thousand men of Israel" (1 Chronicles 21:14).

This exact story can be found in 2 Samuel 24. The two accounts are nearly identical, almost word for word, with one significant difference: the instigator. The 2 Samuel version of this story begins with "the anger of" Yahweh burning "against Israel" (2 Samuel 24:1). He became so angry that "he incited David against them, saying, 'Go and take a census'" (2 Samuel 24:1). With rage in his heart, Yahweh, the perfect Christian deity, told David to commit a sin in order to justify him killing thousands of Israelites out of anger.

Why did Yahweh choose not to punish the one who sinned? What did these seventy thousand Israelites do to deserve Yahweh's fatal penalty? If the Christian deity had a good reason to be angry with the Israelite people, then why did he not punish them for that? Why did he need David to commit a sin? Why does the Christian deity not have more respect for human life?

In both narratives, David was provoked by an outside influence. Satan only interfered once in 1 Chronicles 21:1 and killed zero people. In both versions, Yahweh kills seventy thousand people, and in 2 Samuel 24, the Christian deity himself is the trickster, the one who incites the sin that will cause the punishment. Who is the villain in these stories?

No matter how small the detail, a book ceases to be perfect once it has contradicted itself. The Bible cannot be used as a source of unequivocal truth, while at the same time presenting such a variety of conflicting storylines and ideas. How can anyone find the Bible to be a credible source for answers when it raises way more questions than it can possibly answer? Why would anyone believe the absurdities written inside of an inconsistent book? Why would anyone want to worship the monster described within its pages?

Chapter 3

Confessions of a Deified Child Killer

Most Christians consider Yahweh to be a perfect example of what a loving father is and should be. They believe him to be their father, their heavenly father. To them, their deity can do no wrong. He has their best interests in mind all the time. Yahweh is their moral compass guiding them along their journey through life. They believe he loves them and cares for them as a loving father would love and care for his children.

In Sunday school, we used to sing a song about how much Jesus, the fleshy version of Yahweh, loves the little children. All the children of the world. Regardless of their ethnicity, according to this song, they are all precious in his sight. Where does this idea come from? Why do Christians believe this to be true? Nowhere in the Bible does it state that Yahweh holds any special fondness for little children. This song is not biblically accurate.

By chapter six of the first book in his autobiography to the world, the Christian father figure is ready to wipe out mankind. The Bible says that "all the people on earth had corrupted their ways" (Genesis 6:12). Yahweh's creations had become disobedient, they refused to follow his guidelines for living. They rebelled against their overbearing, self-centered overlord.

Yahweh decided the best way to correct this glitch in the system was by destroying "all life under the heavens" (Genesis 6:17). He needed to eradicate every living thing on the planet because he felt "regret" for having created mankind (Genesis 6:7). There was nothing the loving, all-knowing, Christian deity could do to pacify his own need for everyone to be obedient, for them to bend to his every will. He was going to "destroy both them and the earth" (Genesis 6:13).

It was not only man that stood to perish by inhaling Yahweh's vengeful rainwater. He wanted all of "the animals" to drown as well (Genesis 6:7). The people that Yahweh had created to worship and obey him were not doing what he created them to do. Yahweh failed to produce beings he would be happy with and not want to exterminate. With the exception of "Noah"—a 600-year-old man—his small family, and a bunch of "animals," Yahweh followed through with his genocidal ambitions (Genesis 7:6-8). All life "on the face of the earth was wiped out" (Genesis 7:23).

Where was the love Yahweh had for all of the little children of the world? Why did he want everyone to experience the terror and suffering of being drowned in his wrathful flood? What crime could all of the infants and puppies have possibly committed to be deserving of such a horrible and grotesque end? Why would anyone follow and endorse a being that supports mass extermination as an effective and justifiable means to an end?

Yahweh confesses to another pointless genocide in the book of Exodus. The story begins when Yahweh hears "the Israelites" as they "cry for help because of their slavery" (Exodus 2:23). At this point in time, his special "people" had "lived in Egypt" as slaves for "430 years" (Exodus 12:40). Why did it take so long for Yahweh to hear his people? Were they complaining the entire time, and Yahweh chose to ignore them, or were they content in their slavery up until this point?

Once their complaining was heard, the Christian deity "remembered his covenant with Abraham, with Isaac and with Jacob" (Exodus 2:24). Their cries "for help" triggered his memory (Exodus 2:23). Only after this, did Yahweh grow "concerned about them" (Exodus 2:25). Why did it take them "crying out" to remind the all-knowing Christian deity of his promise to them (Exodus 3:7)? Why did he forget?

As opposed to merely coming down, rescuing the Israelites from their slavery, and introducing himself as the one true deity. Yahweh decided it would be best to send someone else to negotiate the release of his favorite people. The Christian deity refused to speak for himself, so he persuaded a man named Moses to speak for him. Yahweh told his new recruit about his people "crying out because of their slave drivers," and that their cries had just now "reached" him (Exodus 3:7,9). Unable or unwilling "to bring" his "people the Israelites out of Egypt" on his own, Yahweh wanted Moses to talk to the pharaoh for him (Exodus 3:10).

Moses, being a mere mortal with no special abilities, began to doubt that he would be able to "bring the Israelites out of Egypt" (Exodus 3:11). Consumed by his uncertainty, he asked Yahweh to "send someone else" to talk to the pharaoh (Exodus 4:13). This caused Yahweh's "anger" to burn "against Moses" (Exodus 4:14). Ultimately, Yahweh gave into his complaints and promised to send Moses' "brother, Aaron," to do the talking for him (Exodus 4:14). Once Aaron joined the group, Moses, who was initially supposed to do all the talking for Yahweh, was now responsible for carrying the magic "staff" (Exodus 4:17).

Yahweh had to alter his initial plan because Moses, his first choice, was not up to the task. If Yahweh knows everything, how did he not see this coming? If the Christian deity knew Moses would not work out, why did he not start off with Aaron? Why did he get angry with Moses for doing exactly what he knew he was going to do?

On the way to Egypt, Yahweh explained to his traveling companions his plans for the pharaoh and his son. He revealed to them his true intentions. The Christian deity told them he was about to interfere with free will by hardening the heart of the pharaoh so that he would "not let" his "people go" (Exodus 4:21). He gave his friends instructions to inform the Pharaoh that his "firstborn son" was about to die as a punishment for refusing to let the Israelite people go (Exodus 4:23). A refusal that comes from a hardened heart, Yahweh will bestow upon him. The Christian deity openly admits his plot to force this man to make a fatal choice. With the plan set, the three amigos, Moses, Aaron, and Yahweh, set forth for Egypt to free the Israelites and slay the pharaoh's son.

Upon arriving in Egypt, Aaron met with the pharaoh. He told the pharaoh that his deity, Yahweh, demands he let his "people go, so that they may hold a festival" for him "in the wilderness" (Exodus 5:1). Confused by this request, Pharaoh asked, "who" this Yahweh character was (Exodus 5:2). Aaron told Pharaoh that Yahweh was "The God of the Hebrews" and that they should be allowed to "take a three-day journey into the wilderness to offer sacrifices to" him (Exodus 5:3). He warned the pharaoh that if they did not do this, if they did not slaughter animals to their loving deity in the desert, then he might get angry and "strike" them "with plagues or with the sword" (Exodus 5:3). Pharaoh did not want his Israelite slaves to stop "working" (Exodus 5:5). He told Aaron he would not let them go. No miracles were performed by Moses using his magical stick at this meeting, there were no signs of Yahweh's mighty acts of judgment.

After his encounter with Aaron and Moses, the pharaoh decided to punish Yahweh's special people. He ordered his slave drivers to make their work more difficult. He told them the reason the Israelites were crying out was because they were "lazy" (Exodus 5:8). This was all part of Yahweh's perfect plan.

Later, the traveling brothers presented themselves before the pharaoh again. Once there, Aaron grabbed the magical staff, threw it "down in front of Pharaoh and his officials, and it became a snake" (Exodus 7:10). The pharaoh was unimpressed. He called upon his own "magicians," who then "threw down" their own magical staffs, each transforming into "a snake" (Exodus 7:11-12). They were all able to perform the same trick, "but Aaron's staff" was stronger

(Exodus 7:12). It "swallowed up" the snake staffs of the Egyptian magicians (Exodus 7:12). Once his staff finished devouring the others, Aaron asked the pharaoh to let the Israelite "people go, so that they may worship" Yahweh "in the wilderness" (Exodus 7:16). "Pharaoh's heart became hard and he" did "not listen to them, just as" Yahweh "had said" would happen (Exodus 7:13).

During their next visit to the pharaoh, "Moses and Aaron" took their magical staffs "and struck the water of the Nile," immediately turning it "into blood" (Exodus 7:20). Yahweh's plague was a success, "the Egyptians could not drink" the Nile's "water" (Exodus 7:21). Because "the Egyptian magicians did the same things" and "Pharaoh's heart became hard," he would not let Yahweh's people go worship him in the desert (Exodus 7:22).

"Seven days" after his bloody water trick, Yahweh told Moses that it was time to go back before the pharaoh and demand that he let the Israelite "people go" and "worship" him (Exodus 7:25-8:1). When the pharaoh refused again, Aaron stretched out his hand over the waters of Egypt, and the frogs came up and covered the land" (Exodus 8:6). Annoyed with all the frogs, Pharaoh summoned the brothers and told them to "pray to" Yahweh and have him "take the frogs away" (Exodus 8:8). Once gone, he would let the Israelite "people go to offer sacrifices to" their deity (Exodus 8:8). Moses asked Yahweh to remove the plague of "frogs" from the land, and Yahweh "did what Moses asked" (Exodus 8:13). "But when Pharaoh saw that there was relief, he hardened his heart" (Exodus 8:15). He refused to let the Israelites go and kill animals in the desert to offer to their deity.

Yahweh told Moses to "tell Aaron" to "stretch out" his "staff and strike the dust of the ground" (Exodus 8:16). Aaron did as he was told, and "all the dust throughout the land of Egypt became gnats" (Exodus 8:17). Gnats were everywhere, assaulting all the "men and" the "animals" of Egypt. Pharaoh's magicians "tried to produce gnats," as Aaron had done but "could not" (Exodus 8:18). "But Pharaoh's heart was hard, and he would not listen" (Exodus 8:19).

During their next visit, the brothers warned Pharaoh that if he did not let Yahweh's "people go" and worship him, they would "send swarms of flies" down upon the land (Exodus 8:21). Pharaoh ignored their threats, and Yahweh sent down "dense swarms of flies" that "poured into Pharaoh's palace" and "throughout Egypt" (Exodus 8:24). When he had enough of the flies, "Pharaoh summoned Moses and Aaron" (Exodus 8:25). He told them that if they removed the flies, he would let them "sacrifice to" their deity as long as it was "in the land" of Egypt (Exodus 8:25). Moses countered his offer and asked if instead they could "take a three-day journey into the wilderness to offer sacrifices to" their deity (Exodus 8:27). Pharaoh agreed to allow them to "go to offer sacrifices to" their deity "in the wilderness" as long as they did "not go very far" (Exodus 8:28). Once the pharaoh saw that the brothers had removed the plague from Egypt, he "hardened his" own "heart and would not let the people go" (Exodus 8:32).

When the brothers returned to Pharaoh, they told him to let Yahweh's "people go" and "worship" their deity (Exodus 9:1). If he refused them again, Yahweh would send down "a terrible plague" upon all of the Egyptian "livestock" (Exodus 9:1-3). Pharaoh ignored their threats, "and the next day," Yahweh killed "all the livestock" that belonged to "the Egyptians" (Exodus 9:6). The Pharaoh's "heart was unyielding and" he did "not let the people go" (Exodus 9:7).

For his next plague, Yahweh chose "festering boils" (Exodus 9:9). Moses and Aaron "stood before Pharaoh," tossed some "soot…into the air," and the "boils" began (Exodus 9:10). Yahweh made sure his plague affected both the "people and" the innocent "animals throughout the land" (Exodus 9:9). This time, before the pharaoh could admit defeat, Yahweh stepped in and "hardened Pharaoh's heart," causing him to again deny the release of the Israelites (Exodus 9:12).

Why would the Christian deity choose to harden someone's heart? Why did he not set things in motion to make his heart grow three sizes bigger? Christians love a good conversion story. Why not soften the man's heart and have him stand as an example of the love and power of the Christian deity? Why choose death and destruction over mercy and compassion?

There was no need to harden the Pharaoh's heart unless Yahweh did not want him to release the Israelites just yet. Why would the Christian deity want these plagues and punishments to play out? What was he trying to accomplish? Back in Exodus chapter 4, Yahweh confessed his plan from the start was to harden the pharaoh's heart and kill his son. Why does he do this? Why does he prefer to cause so much chaos and death?

Aaron and Moses went to Pharaoh yet again. They asked him to let Yahweh's "people go, so that they may worship" their deity (Exodus 9:13). Pharaoh ignored them and did not release the Israelites. So, "Moses stretched out his" magical "staff toward the sky," and Yahweh "sent thunder and hail, and lightning" that "flashed down to the ground" (Exodus 9:23). "It was the worst storm in all the land of Egypt since it had become a nation" (Exodus 9:24). With the most significant hail storm ever wreaking havoc throughout the land, Pharaoh called for Moses. He told Moses he "had enough" of the "thunder and hail," and that it was time for him and his people to go; he did not wish for them "to stay any longer" (Exodus 9:28). However, just as before, the pharaoh changed his mind at the last minute. The pharaoh "and his officials hardened their" own "hearts" (Exodus 9:34). This is the last time that Pharaoh will make a free choice regarding the release of Yahweh's people.

During his massive hailstorm, Yahweh admitted to Moses that he "raised" Pharaoh "up for this very purpose" (Exodus 9:16). He "hardened" the "heart" of the pharaoh "and the hearts of his officials so that" he could "perform these" miraculous "signs" (Exodus 10:1). The Christian deity wanted to "show" off his "power and" he needed his "name" to "be proclaimed in all the earth" (Exodus 9:16). He wanted the Israelites to "tell" their "children and grandchildren how" he "dealt harshly with the Egyptians and how" he "performed" his "signs among them" (Exodus 10:2). To accomplish this goal, he chose to manipulate the free will of Pharaoh and exterminate countless people.

34

Following Yahweh's historic hail and thunderstorm, Aaron and Moses went to see the Pharaoh. They demanded that he let the Israelite "people go, so that they may worship" Yahweh (Exodus 10:3). Pharaoh, feeling strangely generous, told them that he would allow "only the men" to "go and worship" Yahweh (Exodus 10:11). This was not enough. The pharaoh's compromise did not satisfy the Christian deity. He sent down "locusts" that "invaded all" of "Egypt...in great numbers" (Exodus 10:13-14). The locusts "covered all the ground until it was black" (Exodus 10:15). "They devoured all that was left after the hail" (Exodus 10:15). Again, Pharaoh yielded. He "summoned Moses and Aaron" to take the "plague away" (Exodus 10:16-17). After removing the locusts from Egypt, the pharaoh was ready to allow the Israelites to go and worship their deity, but Yahweh prevented him from doing so. Again, he "hardened Pharaoh's heart," ensuring "he would not let the Israelites go" (Exodus 10:20).

The Christian deity meddles with this man's free will so his creations "may know that" he "is the Lord" (Exodus 10:2). Later, Yahweh declares that he "will gain glory for" himself "through Pharaoh" (Exodus 14:4). He wanted attention. He wanted to be praised for dramatically solving a problem he could have prevented. He allowed his people to be captured. He even forgot about them for a bit. Are these the actions of a loving father figure?

A plague of "darkness that can be felt" was next on Yahweh's list of awful things to do to the Egyptian people (Exodus 10:21). "Moses stretched out his hand toward the sky, and total darkness covered all of Egypt for three days" (Exodus 10:22). When Pharaoh had suffered enough of Yahweh's plague, he "summoned Moses" yet again and told him to "go worship" his deity (Exodus 10:24). This time he permitted the "women and children" to "go," but their "flocks and herds" had to stay "behind" in Egypt (Exodus 10:24).

This was a deal-breaker for Moses. He told Pharaoh that, without their animals, they would not have any "sacrifices" to appease their deity (Exodus 10:25). Their ritualistic slaughter and burnt bodies were needed for "worshiping" Yahweh (Exodus 10:26). Before

Pharaoh had a chance to reply, Yahweh, once again, interfered with free will. He "hardened Pharaoh's heart," so that "he was not willing to let" the Israelite people "go" (Exodus 10:27). Pharaoh did not make his heart hard on his own, nor did he change his mind willingly. Yahweh forced his will upon the pharaoh.

There was "one more plague" to go (Exodus 11:1). Yahweh informed Moses that after the devastation caused by this final plague, Pharaoh would "drive" them "out completely" (Exodus 11:1). The Christian deity was about to personally "pass through Egypt and strike down every firstborn, both people and animals" (Exodus 12:12). Yahweh's plan to let "the Egyptians…know" he was "the Lord" was to execute countless in a single evening, including innocent children, while they slept in their beds (Exodus 14:4).

The Christian deity, not wanting his favorite people to suffer from his pointless show of power, instructed them on how to avoid this plague. To save their households from the irrational actions of their deity, they had to take a "lamb", one "without defect," and on "the fourteenth day of the month…slaughter" it "at twilight" (Exodus 12:5-6). Yahweh wanted them "to take some of the blood" from their slaughtered lambs "and put it on the sides and tops of" their "doorframes" (Exodus 12:7). They were "to eat the meat" of the lamb "roasted over the fire," and if there were any leftovers, they had to "burn" them (Exodus 12:8-10).

Why would an all-knowing, loving deity need a marker to distinguish between two things? And why would he require blood to be that marker? Was Yahweh unable to tell the difference between the houses of his favorite people and those he wished to kill? Why not have them carve an X or smear ash or dung onto the doorframe? Why choose death? Why does Yahweh continue to demand the killing of living creatures for absurd reasons?

As "midnight" arrived in "Egypt," Yahweh crept through the slumbering city. One by one, he entered all the houses that did not have blood on their doors and personally "struck down all the firstborn in Egypt" (Exodus 12:29). "There was not a house without someone dead" inside (Exodus 12:30). Similar to the idea of Santa

Claus, Yahweh entered their homes at night while everyone was asleep. But instead of leaving presents, he left dead babies. Yahweh forced a human to make a choice that would bring about a punishment, not just for that person, but a punishment that would impact an entire population. He exterminated kids in their beds so that his "name might be proclaimed in all the earth" (Exodus 9:16).

Why did Yahweh choose to show off through a series of cruel and pointlessly dramatic methods? What kind of monster uses the deaths of children as evidence for his strength? Yahweh "is in heaven; he does whatever pleases him," and assassinating children was something he wanted to do (Psalm 115:3). If not, he would have chosen a different way to demonstrate his powers.

At some point, "during the night, Pharaoh" discovered his "firstborn" child dead (Exodus 12:29-31). Devastated, he immediately ordered the release of all the Israelite people to go and "worship" their deity just as they had "requested" (Exodus 12:31). But the Christian deity was not through with the pharaoh. In an effort to "gain" more "glory for" himself, Yahweh hardened "Pharaoh's heart," one last time (Exodus 14:4). He discarded his policy of free will and caused this grieving father to change his mind.

The pharaoh grabbed "six hundred of" his "best chariots, along with all the other chariots of Egypt" and pursued the Israelites he had just released (Exodus 14:7). With Pharaoh's entire chariot army quickly gaining ground, Moses and his band of merry men, women, and children found themselves trapped by the Red Sea. Pharaoh had them cornered. Moses, equipped with his magical stick, "stretched out his hand over the sea" and Yahweh "drove" the water "back with a strong east wind and turned it into dry land" (Exodus 14:21). Yahweh "divided" the Red Sea, forming a path for the Israelites to escape (Exodus 14:21-22). Pharaoh and his entire army of chariots "pursued them...into the sea" (Exodus 14:23). Yahweh watched and waited until every last member of Pharaoh's army was on the dry sea bed. Satisfied they had ventured in far enough, Yahweh caused "the wheels of their chariots" to fall off, denying them a rapid retreat (Exodus 14:25).

Once all of his favorite humans had safely made it to shore, Yahweh commanded Moses to finish the job he had started. Moses stretched out his "hand over the sea," and all the water began to "flow back over the Egyptians and their chariots" (Exodus 14:26). Stranded, "Pharaoh" and his "entire army" were swept away "into the sea," and "not one of them survived" (Exodus 14:28). With this final act of violence, Yahweh's pointless genocide was now complete.

Why did Yahweh have to drown all of the horses along with the men? Was Yahweh not capable of saving them? Does he not have the best magic? He could have caused all the horses to fly away to safety or slapped some disposable gills on them so they would not drown. Would that not be a great show of power? Upon witnessing this, would the Israelites not have been impressed with his abilities and his mercy?

It did not matter if the Pharaoh had a change of heart and allowed the Israelites to go worship their deity. Yahweh's plan was to ignore free will and rain down death and terror upon the Egyptian people. He wanted to be seen as powerful and relevant. He determined the best way to acquire the fame and recognition he so desperately sought was to kill countless living beings. The loving Christian deity is willing to kill children to get attention.

Following his pre-meditated mass killings in Egypt, Yahweh's anger and wrath began to grow toward a group of people called the Amalekites. The first time Yahweh's favorite people came into contact with "the Amalekites" was in the book of Exodus, when they "attacked the Israelites," seemingly without instigation (Exodus 17:8). During this battle, Moses stood "on top of" a "hill" with his magical staff raised high (Exodus 17:9). "As long as Moses held up his hands, the Israelites" would continue to win the battle (Exodus 17:11). "But whenever he lowered his hands, the Amalekites" would begin to win (Exodus 17:11). Eventually, the Israelites were victorious and "overcame the Amalekite army with the sword" (Exodus 17:13).

Yahweh had the power to wipe out this army. He could have intervened in countless ways. Instead of preventing the deaths of his beloved people altogether, he chose to have the battle play out. Why? Because he wanted to watch Moses hold a stick in the air. He wanted his servants to do something ridiculous to prove his loyalty to him.

Once the battle ended, Yahweh stated he would "completely blot out the name of Amalek from under heaven," thus removing the Amalekite people from memory (Exodus 17:14). He "then" told "Moses" to "write" down his encounter with the Amalekites "on a scroll as something to be remembered" for "Joshua" (Exodus 17:14). Writing down a memory of someone, as something to be remembered later on, completely defeats the purpose of trying to remove them from memory. Yahweh does not want anyone to remember these people, but he had it written down so that these people would be remembered. It boggles the mind how anyone can find this book or the deity described within its pages to be perfect.

Long after their first encounter, Yahweh remembered the Amalekite people and "what they did to Israel" (1 Samuel 15:2). In retaliation against "the Amalekites" for attacking his favorite people way back in the book of Exodus, Yahweh sent the Israelite army to "totally destroy" everything that belonged to "the Amalekites" (1 Samuel 15:3). He ordered his army to kill all of the Amalekite "men and women, children and infants, cattle and sheep, camels and donkeys" (1 Samuel 15:3). According to the Christian deity, his desire for vengeance against these people gave him the authority to start slaughtering their women and children.

Why would the loving Christian deity order the deaths of infants? Why does he need the children to die? If the argument is that the children would grow up to become enemies of the Israelite people, then why not give them a change of heart? Is the Christian deity unwilling to manipulate the heart of a child to save their life? If he is willing to change the heart of the pharaoh to show off his powers, why is he not willing to change the heart of a child to save them from the sword? With countless options available to him, the Christian deity chooses to order the killing of all the children and infants.

By his own admission, through his own breathed out words, Yahweh tells us that he is a "jealous" deity who punishes "children for the sin of the parents" (Exodus 20:5). Fueled by his uncontrollable jealousy, the Christian deity chooses to punish the children of these transgressors, those who did no wrong, until "the third and fourth generation" (Exodus 20:5). Why does he hold on to his anger for so long? Would your idea of the perfect father get all jealous and overreact with an exaggerated punishment if their kid started paying more attention to someone else's dad? This is not what a perfect, loving father looks like.

Yahweh cannot contain his rage when his favorite people "bow down to" or "worship" other deities (Exodus 20:5). When he finds out they have made "idols or set up an image or sacred stone for" themselves, the demigod lashes out irrationally (Leviticus 26:1). He demands they worship at his feet and no one else's. They are to observe his "Sabbaths and have reverence for" his "sanctuary" (Leviticus 26:2).

If the Israelites were "careful to obey" all of his "commands," Yahweh would "send" them "rain in its season," causing "the ground" to "yield its crops" (Leviticus 26:3-4). In exchange for their obedience, Yahweh promised them "all the food" they could ever want to eat (Leviticus 26:5). He ensured them "safety" by removing both "sword" and "wild beasts from the land" (Leviticus 26:5-6). He would do all of these things as long as they were subservient and worshiped him exclusively.

"But if" the Israelite people did "not listen to" Yahweh and if they failed to "carry out all" of his "commands," he promised to "bring on" them "sudden terror, wasting diseases and fever" that would "destroy" their "sight and" drain away their lives (Leviticus 26:14-16). He would allow them to "be defeated by" their "enemies" (Leviticus 26:17). He would cause their "soil" to "not yield its crops" (Leviticus 26:20). And, if they still refused "to listen to" the Christian deity, he would "send wild animals" to "rob" them of their "children" (Leviticus 26:21-22). Comply and submit, or Yahweh will personally send wild animals to tear your children apart.

"If in spite of" these things, they still did "not listen to" Yahweh, his "anger" would cause him to become even more "hostile toward" them (Leviticus 26:27-28). He would decide to make them "eat the flesh of" their children (Leviticus 26:29). Unable or unwilling to bridle his anger, Yahweh chose to force people to eat their children as a punishment. He did this on several occasions.

In the book of Deuteronomy, Yahweh again explains the benefits he has waiting for those who "fully obey...all his commands" (Deuteronomy 28:1). For their unfaltering allegiance, they "will be blessed in the city and blessed in the country" (Deuteronomy 28:3). "However, if" the Israelite people did "not obey" Yahweh, he would bring "curses" upon them (Deuteronomy 28:15). He would cause them to "eat the fruit of the womb, the flesh of" their "sons and daughters" (Deuteronomy 28:53).

According to the book of Ezekiel, Yahweh was upset because his special city, Jerusalem, had "rebelled against" his "laws and decrees" (Ezekiel 5:6). He decided that he was going to "inflict punishment on" them (Ezekiel 5:8). He would "send famine and wild beasts against" the people of Jerusalem in an effort to "leave" them "childless" (Ezekiel 5:17). The Christian deity wanted all the disloyal "parents" to "eat their" own "children" (Ezekiel 5:10). Through this act of adolescent cannibalism, Yahweh believed he would "be avenged" (Ezekiel 5:13).

According to the book of Isaiah, the Israelite people were not seeking out Yahweh, so he threatened to have them "feed on the flesh of their own offspring" (Isaiah 9:20). The book of Jeremiah says, because the "people of Jerusalem" did not worship Yahweh exclusively evidenced by their "burned" sacrifices to "foreign gods," he promised to make them "eat the flesh of their" children (Jeremiah 19:3-9). In retaliation against his own people for not listening to his commands, as a means of seeking revenge for his hurt feelings, Yahweh sought to use the cannibalizing of one's own children as a punishment. This was something he wanted to do, something he found to be effective. Why would a loving deity want anyone to eat a child? Do these demands and consequences sound like the actions of a loving father?

The book of Hosea describes the Tribe of Ephraim. In Genesis, "Ephraim" is revealed as the son of Joseph (Genesis 46:20). "Ephraim," had been found "guilty of Baal worship and died (Hosea 13:1). The Bible says the people of Ephraim began to "sin more and more (Hosea 13:2). They were kissing "calf-idols" and offering up "human sacrifices" (Hosea 13:2). To Yahweh, the worst of it was that they disobeyed his command to "acknowledge no God but" him (Hosea 13:4). "Because of their sinful deeds," Yahweh "no longer" loved "them" (Hosea 9:15). He "hated" these people for their betrayal (Hosea 9:15).

The Christian deity decided the best way to handle this situation was to "slay their cherished offspring" (Hosea 9:16). With vengeance in his heart, Yahweh cursed the Tribe of Ephraim. He allowed them "no birth, no pregnancy," and "no conception" (Hosea 9:11). He cursed the "wombs" of all their pregnant women, causing them to "miscarry" (Hosea 9:14).

Forcing abortions and sterilizing women was not enough to subdue Yahweh's hatred and jealousy. He wanted these people and their children to suffer greatly. The loving Christian deity chose to make all of their "breasts" run "dry," leaving countless infants to wither away and starve (Hosea 9:14). He wanted all of their kids to die. "Even if they" were to "bear children," he would "slay" them (Hosea 9:16). Again, Yahweh chose death instead of life. Senseless slaughter instead of love and compassion.

According to the book of Jeremiah, "the people of Anathoth" angered Yahweh by worshiping other deities (Jeremiah 11:21). One day, he decided it was time to "bring disaster on" them (Jeremiah 11:23). Yahweh chose to "punish them" by causing "their young men" to "die by the sword" and "their sons and daughters by famine" (Jeremiah 11:22). The adults were giving attention to someone else, so Yahweh starved their kids. He "does whatever pleases him" (Psalm 135:6). He wanted these children to suffer and die for the sins of their fathers, or he would have chosen another form of punishment.

Death by starvation is a prolonged and painful process. Have you ever been so hungry that it hurt? Now imagine not being able to suppress that hunger, not being able to fill your stomach and stop that pain. The loving Christian deity sat up in his cloud, looking down at the children as they slowly starved to death, feeling satisfied that his punishment upon them was just and deserving. Yahweh believes that if you love or praise any deity that is not him, then that gives him the freedom to kill whoever he wants as a repercussion for that act. Worship only me or I'll kill your children. Listen to me, or I'll kill your children. These are not the demands of a loving father.

Yahweh chose to torture and kill the children of those he hated, demonstrating that he does not hate the sin, but actually the sinner. He hates them so much that he slaughtered their kids. This is the same deity currently being endorsed around the world as an example of a loving and perfect parent.

The book of 2 Kings recounts the story of Elisha and his cursed bears. One day "Elisha" was out for a walk in "Bethel" minding his own business, when out of nowhere, "some boys" began to mock him for his appearance (2 Kings 2:23). They were calling him "baldy" (2 Kings 2:23). This was too much for Elisha. "He turned around…and called down a curse on them in the name of" Yahweh (2 Kings 2:24). The Christian deity did not have to follow through with this curse. He must have felt these little kids needed to pay for their insulting words because he either cursed or allowed to be cursed "two bears," that "came out of the woods" and "mauled forty-two of the" children (2 Kings 2:24). This was how the Christian deity decided to retaliate against a bunch of kids who merely mocked his prophet.

If a child makes fun of his father's boss, are they thrown to a group of cursed bears for doing so? How can anyone see that as a justifiable punishment? Is this how people living in a civilized society would behave? Is this how a perfect father would react?

Yahweh believes that foolishness "is bound up in the heart of a child, but the rod of discipline will drive it far away" (Proverbs 22:15). "If someone has a stubborn and rebellious son," the Christian deity wants the parents to take the insubordinate child to "all the men of his town" and "stone him to death" (Deuteronomy

21:18-21). As opposed to merely grounding him or sending him to a time out, Yahweh preferred to have the child "put to death" (Leviticus 20:9). Jesus reiterates the commands of his Old Testament counterpart in the book of Mark. He told a group of people that "anyone who curses their father or mother is to be put to death" (Mark 7:9-10). Yahweh sees this as a perfectly reasonable and rational thing to do. He has no issue with kids being hit with rocks until they have suffered enough blows to the body and head that they stop moving. He wants their lives to be painfully extinguished for their insubordination. These are not the commands of a compassionate being.

In the book of Hosea, "the people of Samaria...rebelled against" the Christian deity (Hosea 13:16). Because of this, Yahweh felt he had no other choice but to cause "their little ones" to "be dashed to the ground," and "their pregnant women" to be "ripped open" (Hosea 13:16). In the book of Psalm, Yahweh talks of a happiness his people got from seizing the "infants" of his enemies and hitting "them against the rocks" (Psalm 137:9). What kind of monster cheerfully bashes children against rocks? There is no respect for human life shone to these innocent women and children. How is this behavior acceptable to a loving being?

The book of Judges contains the story of a man named "Jephthah, the Gileadite," who "was a mighty warrior" (Judges 11:1). One day, "the elders of Gilead" came to him with a proposition (Judges 11:5). They wanted Jephthah to be their "commander" for their upcoming "fight" with "the Ammonites" (Judges 11:6). Jephthah agreed to help them and took the job. After sending messages back and forth to "the king of the Ammonites," Jephthah "made a vow to" Yahweh that if Yahweh would deliver "the Ammonites into" his hands, then anything that came "out of the door of" his "house to meet" him when he returned "in triumph," would be Yahweh's, and Jephthah would "sacrifice it as a burnt offering" to him (Judges 11:12-31).

"The Spirit of" Yahweh possessed "Jephthah," as he "advanced against the Ammonites," (Judges 11:29). Yahweh tipped the battle in Jephthah's favor delivering "the Ammonites into" his "hands" (Judges 11:32). "When Jephthah returned to his home in Mizpah, who should come out to meet him but his daughter, dancing to the sound of tambourines! She was only a child" (Judges 11:34). What did Jephthah think was going to come out of his house to meet him, some chickens, his favorite goat? Did he not expect a family member to be the first one to greet him upon his return home from war? Usually, the kids are the ones who come running out first. He must have known this.

Jephthah had no choice. He had made a deal, "a vow to the" Christian deity to burn whatever came through the door to greet him (Judges 11:35). Without interference or objection from the loving Christian deity, Jephthah "did as he had vowed" (Judges 11:39). Yahweh watched as Jephthah took his daughter, tied her up, and set her on fire as a thank you for granting him victory in battle against the Ammonites. A human child was sacrificed to the Christian deity, and not once did he say it was something to be condemned, or never to be repeated.

The book of 2 Samuel contains the story of David and Bathsheba. Most are familiar with David's indiscretions with his bathing neighbor. However, most are not familiar with the details of what happened after the affair took place. How was David punished for his sinful act? How did Yahweh choose to retaliate against one of his all-time favorite people?

The story begins with David pacing "around on the roof of the palace," unable to sleep. (2 Samuel 11:2). While looking into random windows, "he saw a woman bathing" (2 Samuel 11:2). He liked what he saw so much that "he sent someone to find out" more "about her" (2 Samuel 11:3). "The man" David had asked, knew who the woman was (2 Samuel 11:3). He said her name was "Bathsheba" and that she was "the wife of Uriah the Hittite" (2 Samuel 11:3). Undeterred by her marital status, "David sent messengers to get her" (2 Samuel 11:4). She was brought into his bedroom, "and he slept with her" (2 Samuel 11:4).

This one act of adultery, this one sin, had a particular price. Yahweh set a very specific punishment for adulterers way back in the book of Leviticus. He demanded that "both the adulterer and the adulteress...be put to death" (Leviticus 20:10). The Christian deity makes it very clear that no one gets to survive an adulterous act. Yet neither David nor Bathsheba were killed for this sin.

Yahweh chose to punish David by taking all of his "wives" away from him (2 Samuel 12:11). Bathsheba completely avoided her punishment. She found a loophole by somehow "purifying herself from her...uncleanness" (2 Samuel 11:4). Both managed to escape the mandated consequences of their actions.

Bathsheba found herself "pregnant" with David's child (2 Samuel 11:5). Hesitant to tell her husband about her encounter with the king, she "sent word to David," telling him that he was going to be a father (2 Samuel 11:5). Troubled by this news, David devised a plan.

David sent for Bathsheba's husband, Uriah, who was fighting in a battle against "the Ammonites" (2 Samuel 11:1). Initially, his idea was to have Bathsheba's husband come back home and have some of that you-made-it-home-from-battle-alive sex with his wife. Thus, explaining the new baby and clearing David of any future fatherly duties. However, when "Uriah" arrived, he did not go home to his wife. Instead, he "slept at the entrance to the palace" (2 Samuel 11:9). The next morning when "David" found that "Uriah did not go home," he got upset (2 Samuel 11:10). "Uriah" would not go home to his "wife" while all of his army buddies were "camped in the open country" (2 Samuel 11:11). He would "not do such a thing" (2 Samuel 11:11). For his second attempt, "David" tried to get "Uriah" drunk, but still, "he did not go home" (2 Samuel 11:13). David had run out of options. Uriah had left him with no choice. David was going to have to kill Uriah to cover up the adultery.

In the morning, David drafted a letter to one of his captains. He told this captain to "put Uriah out...where the fighting" was the "fiercest" (2 Samuel 11:15). David wanted them to take him out and "withdraw from him," causing poor "Uriah" to "be struck down" (2

Samuel 11:15). Uriah carried the letter containing the orders from David back to the battlefield, unknowingly delivering instructions for his own downfall.

"Joab," David's military captain, received the message and sent "Uriah" out to "a place where he knew the strongest defenders" would be (2 Samuel 11:16). "Uriah the Hittite" did not survive (2 Samuel 11:17). He died because his king found his wife attractive and took her into his bed. Uriah's only crime was his wife's beauty. When Bathsheba heard that Uriah had fallen in battle, she "mourned" the death of "her husband" (2 Samuel 11:26). "David" waited until "after the time of mourning was over," and then "had her brought to his house" to become his "wife" (2 Samuel 11:27).

David betrayed and murdered a man in order to hide his own sin. Murder is another one of those sins that Yahweh has set to be punishable by death. Yahweh's rule states that if "anyone…takes the life of a human being," they must "be put to death" (Leviticus 24:17). David was directly responsible for Uriah's death, but again escaped the fatal penalty his deity had put in place. Yahweh took "away" David's "sin," and because of this, "David" was "not going to die" for it (2 Samuel 12:13). The Christian deity chose instead to punish David's family with "the sword" (2 Samuel 12:10). Yahweh's anger did not burn against David, he did not send cursed bears to maul him, or a flood to drown him for what he had done. The Christian deity was merely "displeased" by David's unlawful actions (2 Samuel 11:27). The king of Israel committed adultery and, in an attempt to cover it up, ordered the death of a loyal soldier. This is "a man after" Yahweh's "own heart," this is the man that did "everything" the Christian deity wanted "him to do" (Acts 13:22).

David's sin had been forgiven, but his actions were not forgotten by Yahweh's enemies. They showed "utter contempt" after David's transgressions (2 Samuel 12:14). The Christian deity sought revenge for his wounded ego. He chose to kill David's "son" in retaliation (2 Samuel 12:14).

Consumed by his irrational need for vengeance, the Christian deity "struck the child that Uriah's wife had borne to David, and he became ill" (2 Samuel 12:15). "On the seventh day" of this Yahweh-given sickness, "the child died" (2 Samuel 12:18). Not satisfied with just killing the child outright, the Christian deity wanted him to suffer for seven days before dying of the illness he so lovingly bestowed upon him. This was not by accident, nor was his hand forced. Yahweh was disrespected by his enemies, so he thought it would be a great idea to retaliate by torturing a child for a week before killing him.

If the Bible is true, then Yahweh "knows everything," past, present, and future (1 John 3:20). He knew David would sin before he did it. He knew his enemies were going to disrespect him because of that sin. And he knew he was going to torture and kill David's innocent child in response to that disrespect. He wanted this to happen. He planned it all out.

To what end is a child's suffering and death of any value? The Bible is littered with pointless acts of savagery and barbarism brought forth by the loving Christian deity against those who have done nothing wrong. He drowns them. He slaughters them. He sends wild animals to rip them apart. Yahweh's past is stained with the blood of countless innocent children.

Christians believe their deity is the good guy, the hero. Have you ever seen the hero go around and kill a bunch of kids? Does he drown them out of frustration? Would he threaten to feed someone's children to wild animals? These are obviously not the characteristics of a hero. Villains threaten and harm the innocent. They are the ones who go around causing death and destruction, not the hero. How do Christians not see Yahweh for the villain he portrays himself to be in the Bible?

Most Christians, when asked to demonstrate how their deity is loving, will point to that one time when he sent his own child to Earth to be the ultimate sacrifice to himself. How is that a loving act? Love comes out of empathy and kindness. Not sending one's own child to die because you chose not to forgive people "without the shedding of blood" (Hebrews 9:22). This is not an example of love.

Most Christians believe the Bible contains the documented acts of Yahweh. If these stories are factual, then the Christian deity really did slaughter and starve all those kids. Christians will use their holy book to justify their claims of Yahweh's loving nature, completely ignoring the verses that speak of his misplaced violence and hatred. They will pick out the parts they like and focus on those verses or ideas, ignoring everything they do not understand or cannot defend. Many never bother to even read the whole book. They hone in on their personal view of Yahweh and find verses to support it.

Even if they do admit their deity kills children, Christians will never say he was wrong to do so. It does not matter how many innocent children Yahweh slaughters because, in their eyes, he must have had a good reason. Tell me, is there ever a good reason to torture and kill a child? Yahweh thinks there is. He gives us several reasons and situations that he uses to justify the torture and killing of kids. The Bible says Yahweh killed children in droves and that he had no remorse for his actions. We "are regarded as nothing," Yahweh "does as he pleases with the powers of heaven and the peoples of the earth" (Daniel 4:35).

In reality, Christians willingly and wholeheartedly worship a documented child killer. They want you and your children to bow down in reverence to this being. They want the whole world to worship and be subservient to him. Why would anyone idolize someone that kills children? Why would anyone want to worship such a monster?

Chapter 4

Prayer is Not a Verb

Dictionary.com defines prayer as "a spiritual communion with a god or an object of worship." This means prayer can be used to communicate with any deity, ancient relative, or inanimate object of your choosing. Prayer offers the Christian a unique opportunity to converse with their creator deity. The Bible says when one prays to Yahweh, he "is near" (Deuteronomy 4:7). Most Christians believe their deity listens empathetically and intently to their every word.

However, for most Christians, Yahweh does not respond to their prayers immediately with a physical voice, assuring them that their prayer has indeed been heard. Instead, Yahweh says nothing. This leaves the Christian with nothing more than a hope that their prayer has been heard and will be answered in a timely fashion. In reality, there is no difference between wishing upon a star, throwing a coin down a well, or a prayer to Yahweh.

Some Christians believe that their deity will send down a sign or a clue to let them know his decision on their prayer request or which path in life he wants them to take. Without a positive confirmation from Yahweh, Christians who claim to see a sign are the ones who are interpreting these heavenly hints as an answer to their prayers. It is the Christian alone confirming the validity and purpose of these signs. They must decide if their deity is attempting to communicate through inanimate objects or random occurrences such as a tornado changing course or a beam of light shining through the clouds. There is no way to conclude that it is, in fact, their deity's answer to their prayers. There is no way to discern between their own thoughts and desires and their deity's supposed response. Christians have to establish some sort of unique way of deciphering the answers they seek from a mute deity. Without an audible verification from Yahweh, how does a Christian know without a doubt that it is their deity showing them the right path and not their own wishes or biased belief structure?

If I pray for a sign that I should move to another state, and I start to see the name of that state everywhere, is that a sign that I should move there? Or was the state's name simply everywhere already, and I had not noticed it until I was looking for a sign? If Yahweh can make it so that I see a particular state everywhere, he can tell me in a non-mysterious way where he would like me to move. A physical voice would be helpful. An actual sign that reads, "Hey, move here," would also be useful.

What if I applied to a job and prayed to get hired? If I got hired, what was the most likely the reason? Was it me and my work history or an invisible, omniscient being that persuaded them to hire me? Christians will see it as an intervention rather than the simple confirmation bias that it is.

Christians, when answering for their inaudible deity, are asserting to know his mind, his way of thinking. They claim to know his thoughts and desires. Their will becomes his will, their biases become his biases. The mind of the theist is the mind of their own deity. They control his thoughts and actions. It is in the brain of the devoted follower that their personal deity resides.

Some Christians believe they have heard their deity respond with a physical voice. Some claim they are able to carry on full-blown two-way conversations with him. This is called an auditory hallucination. Hearing voices can be a sign of something more serious. I am not saying that all Christians who hear Yahweh talking to them are schizophrenic. But, if you or someone you know does hear voices, please seek the appropriate professional for help. Schizophrenia is a serious condition that can be harmful to the person with the disorder and pose a threat to those around them.

Occasionally, Christians use prayer as a way to thank their deity for an action they believe he is directly responsible for. Yet, more commonly, these prayers are used to ask Yahweh for things they want or need. They ask for money, a promotion at work, or that miracle cure. They request angelic protection during their travels. They will even ask to have their food blessed. The list of requests is often as endless as it is pointless.

If their caring, all-knowing, all-powerful deity wanted to do something for them, he would do it, regardless of them asking. If the Christian deity does not know everything, then there might be an argument for the need to pray. But Yahweh clearly states that he knows everything. So, why would a Christian, who believes that their loving, caring deity already knows what they need and want, need to ask for anything? Would not his all-knowingness make the prayer, the asking for something part, completely unnecessary? If my kids are hungry, I feed them. If my children need protection or guidance, I don't wait until they get on their hands and knees begging.

Further complicating the concept of prayer, Yahweh states in the book of Jeremiah that he knows "the plans" he has "for you" (Jeremiah 29:11). If the Christian deity knows everything and already has a set plan for everyone, what good would it do to pray and ask him to change these plans? Imagine buying a plane ticket to Las Vegas, and while in mid-flight, you ask the pilot to take a detour to Hawaii. You demand a change in course from the already determined path. The same concept applies to the Christian deity. Praying for something you want to happen is a pointless act if your deity already has a set way that things are going to go.

Where does the idea to bless one's food before eating it come from? As a kid, I was never allowed to touch my food until someone prayed over it. Even when out in public at a crowded restaurant, not one bite could be eaten until the entire table held hands, bowed their heads, and blessed the meal in front of them. Not once does the Bible instruct or require someone to pray over their food before they eat it. According to the book of Deuteronomy, Yahweh wants his people to praise him "for the good land he has given" to them, after they eat their meals, not before (Deuteronomy 8:10). He wants to be recognized for his contribution of creation, without which there would be no food to eat in the first place.

Jesus never actually prays over his food, but he does thank Yahweh for it on three separate occasions. The first time Jesus thanks Yahweh for his food, occurs in the book of Matthew, when he feeds five thousand men, plus all the women and children, with only "five loaves of bread and two fish" (Matthew 14:17). He was able to accomplish this impossible feat after he "gave thanks" to Yahweh (Matthew 14:19). Jesus repeats this performance later on when he feeds four thousand men, plus all the women and children, with only "seven" "loaves" of bread "and a few small fish" (Matthew 15:34). Again, Jesus was only able to multiply the bread and fish after "he had given thanks" to Yahweh for it (Matthew 15:36). The third and final time the Bible records the Christian demigod being thankful for his food occurs in the book of Luke. Jesus, freshly resurrected from the dead, "took bread, gave thanks," and passed it out to all those who were sitting at the table with him (Luke 24:30). Once they touched or ate the enchanted bread, "their eyes were opened and they recognized him" just before "he disappeared from their sight" (Luke 24:31). Jesus was able to give the bread special abilities after he had given thanks.

Is there some kind of connection between thanking Yahweh for your food and the ability to enhance or multiply that food? Do Christians believe that if they thank Yahweh for their meals that it will change their food in any way? What do they think will happen if they forget to bless it and take a bite? Will Yahweh refuse to nourish their bodies with it? Will it increase the likelihood of choking or food poisoning? Predictably, the Bible is unclear on how it all works.

Christians will often use prayer as a way to ask Yahweh to send supernatural support or comfort to people in times of hardship. They pass the responsibility to help someone onto their deity, leaving the person the prayer is supposed to help, often without any help at all.

Contrary to popular belief, prayer is actually a noun. Many Christians replace physical assistance with thoughts and prayers. Sending thoughts and prayers does nothing but make the person sending them feel like they did something to help out. It leaves those who are hungry still in need of food, and those who are sick and dying still sick and dying. Prayer should never be used as a replacement for actual physical assistance or support.

In the book of Matthew, Yahweh informs his people as to where he would like them to do their praying. Yahweh tells them "not" to "be like the hypocrites" who "love to pray standing in the synagogues and on the street corners to be seen by others" (Matthew 6:5). Instead, the Bible instructs the believer to "go into" their "room, close the door and pray" by themselves (Matthew 6:6). Yahweh wants his people to pray in private. Not at a flagpole, not on national television, not at a busy restaurant, and definitely not at your son's soccer game.

When a Christian asks Yahweh for a favor, they expect results. Their demigod in sandals tells them in the book of Matthew that "if two" or more believers "agree about anything they ask for, it will be done" (Matthew 18:19). In the book of Mark, he claims that if they believe they "have received it," then "whatever" they "ask for in prayer…will be" theirs (Mark 11:24). Their own Bible tells them all their prayers will be answered and that the power of their wishful thinking will somehow give these prayers more potency.

Often times, a Christian will pray for results but not see any. They will beg for help and not receive it. This happens because Yahweh added some fine print to Jesus' claim that anything you want, just ask, and you shall receive. Apparently, the Christian deity must first pre-approve a wish before granting it. As long as what they are asking for is something that is "according to his will," he will acknowledge their request (1 John 5:14). Prayer only works if Yahweh wants it to. The addition of "according to his will" negates anything you would selfishly ask for, voiding countless prayers in the process.

Keeping a child alive and cancer-free can be viewed as selfish to some Christians. Yahweh wants the child in heaven, and who are you to question his authority? If he wants your child to suffer and die from cancer, then your prayers for a savior are pointless. This is Yahweh's will for your child and his plans negate any hopes for a happy, healthy, fulfilled life. Good or bad, happy or sad, Yahweh is the one who gets to decide your fate.

Yahweh will look the other way while parents across the world cry out for him to save their dying children. He will allow for the suffering of countless kids, yet grant the wish of a parent asking for their child to sleep well without any complications or nightmares. Why would the Christian deity choose not to save the kid painfully dying of cancer, but choose to help the one next door have pleasant dreams? Why would a loving being comfort one child and watch the other die slowly? Yahweh "is in heaven; he does whatever pleases him" (Psalm 115:3). Why would anyone want to worship such a monster?

Chapter 5

The She is Silent

Most Christian women claim to have a personal relationship with their creator deity. They believe he loves them and cares for them. They think he knows everything about them, their fears, their thoughts, their wants, and their needs. They believe he keeps them from harm and knows what is best for them. But why do they think this? Have they not read their own Bibles? Have they not studied the thoughts, the very breathed out words, of the deity they claim to have a personal relationship with? What I see when I look inside their holy book, is an ignorant, sexist deity with anger issues. I struggle to find a being that cares for its creations, especially women.

Our journey down this rabbit hole of misogyny starts in the Old Testament, in the book of Leviticus. Yahweh, revolted by the natural female monthly "flow of blood," lays out some ground rules for women (Leviticus 15:19). He explains how a single woman, who is on her period, can infect an entire town with an extremely contagious sin hidden inside of her vaginal blood. He instructs his creations on the proper way of handling this bloody situation. Seemingly unaware of the reason for and cause of this natural flow, the Christian deity believes women to be impure, staining the very environment around them during this time. Yahweh believes that the uncleanliness brought on by a woman's period can be spread to "anyone who touches her" (Leviticus 15:19). Even if someone has contact with "anything she was sitting on," that person becomes infected with the invisible sinful cooties, causing them to be "unclean" until the "evening" (Leviticus 15:23). "If a man has sexual relations with" a woman during her period, "he will be unclean for seven days," and everything he touches "will be unclean" (Leviticus 15:24). The spread of this unholy contaminant knows no limits.

Once a woman has finished upsetting the Christian deity with her natural monthly cycle, he requires her to apologize for this offensive function of the female body. He wants her to bring "two doves or two young pigeons" to be sacrificed, "one for a sin offering and the other for a burnt offering" (Leviticus 15:29-30). Yahweh believes that a woman should "make atonement for…the uncleanness of her discharge," by killing birds (Leviticus 15:30). This is the way Yahweh wants things to be done; these are the ridiculous rules he came up with.

Why does Yahweh need payment in the form of death? Why does he seek forgiveness from someone whose body is merely operating the way, he himself, their creator, designed it to operate? A woman is shamed, and animals must die. All because the Christian deity demands to be compensated for the wrong a woman has committed through this completely natural event that she has no control over.

Yahweh feels repulsed by a woman's vaginal bleeding regardless of the cause. Even the blood associated with childbirth is considered unnaturally impure and must be atoned for. If "a woman…gives birth to a son," she is deemed to be "unclean" for a whole week (Leviticus 12:2). She then has to "wait thirty-three days to be purified from her bleeding" (Leviticus 12:4). After giving "birth to a daughter," Yahweh believes she is "unclean" for "two weeks" (Leviticus 12:5). He then wants her to wait an extra "sixty-six days" before he will allow her "to be purified from her bleeding" (Leviticus 12:5). "When the days of her purification" come to an end, Yahweh requires her to bring him a "lamb for a burnt offering and a young pigeon or a dove for a sin offering" (Leviticus 12:6). Yahweh wants women "to make atonement," to apologize to him, for having their natural "flow of blood" (Leviticus 12:7). "These are the regulations" the Christian deity has set for a "woman who gives birth" (Leviticus 12:7). Yahweh believes the natural vaginal bleeding of women is sinful and contagious until an adequate amount of time has passed. Once their offensive flow has stopped, he requires them to kill small animals as an apology to him. People worship this deity. They think you should too.

Yahweh, the supposed creator of women, fails to comprehend how they work. He acts like a child grossed out and afraid of something he does not understand. If he created women from scratch, then he would know why they bleed. Women and their bodily functions should not be a mystery to him. This is the way he made them; it is not their fault.

Yahweh claims this list of menstrual warnings is to keep his people safe "from things that make them unclean" (Leviticus 15:31). To save them from his misplaced wrath. If a cootie carrier enters Yahweh's perfect house, he will kill them. The Christian deity demands that his people be unblemished when they enter his room. The Bible says that Yahweh will kill any Israelite who is caught "defiling" his "dwelling place" with "their uncleanness" (Leviticus 15:31). Yahweh presents himself as a neat freak with a murderous disposition.

According to the book of Leviticus, "if a priest's daughter" becomes "a prostitute," Yahweh wants her to "be burned in the fire" for the disgrace she has brought upon "her father" (Leviticus 21:9). Because a man was embarrassed and ashamed of his daughter's profession, the loving Christian deity wants her to be burned alive. Like so many of the penalties, Yahweh dishes out in the Bible, the punishment for the crime is extreme and completely unnecessary. Curiously though, nothing is said about what should be done if the son of a priest decides to become a prostitute.

When living in a civilized society, certain things like rape are grossly frowned upon. This is something we as a race of beings, for the most part, have decided is a horrific act and should be outlawed. Even we sinful, broken creatures have figured out that raping someone is not a good thing. Yahweh never forbids rape. The divinely inspired Christian handbook for life does not clarify that rape is a

58

bad thing and that one should never engage in such a hideous act. He does, however, make sure you know how he wants you to handle the situation if it comes up.

The book of Deuteronomy details what the Christian deity will and will not tolerate when it comes to the act of rape. "If a man happens to meet in a town a virgin pledged to be married and he sleeps with her," Yahweh wants them both to be stoned "to death" (Deuteronomy 22:23-24). The Christian deity wants the man to die because he took what did not belong to him and "violated another man's wife," while the woman must die because no one heard her "scream for help" (Deuteronomy 22:24). The Christian deity requires women to die for not making enough noise while being raped.

"If a man happens to meet a virgin who is not pledged to be married and rapes her," Yahweh wants the man to pay the girl's father "fifty shekels" and then "marry" her (Deuteronomy 22:28-29). The Christian deity forces women to marry the men who sexually assaulted them. He then demands she "submit to" her husband, "in everything" (Ephesians 5:24). Her loving deity leaves her no choice, she must spend the rest of her life being subservient to her rapist.

The Bible says that the Christian deity granted his fighting men special privileges whenever they went "to war" (Deuteronomy 21:10). If they noticed "a beautiful woman" among their "captives," Yahweh permitted them to "take her as" their "wife" (Deuteronomy 21:11). Again, Yahweh leaves no option for these women. He gives the men complete control over them. They are objects, prizes to be won. Once selected, the woman must "shave her head" and mourn the loss of her family and friends "for a full month" (Deuteronomy 21:12-13). After her month has expired, the man, her abductor, "may go to her and be her husband" (Deuteronomy 21:13).

What kind of monster traps a woman into a relationship with a man that slaughtered her family and friends? Imagine for a moment that you are a woman living in a city that's being attacked by Yahweh's army. These soldiers come into your house, kill your entire family in front of you, and then take you prisoner. While being transported to your cage, you catch the eye of one of the soldiers, and he tells you that you are going to become his wife. You do not have a choice, no one cares what you think, this deplorable act has been cleared by Yahweh, and you must now spend the rest of your life being subservient to the man that murdered your family. These are not the laws and regulations of a loving, competent being.

Most Christians are familiar with the basic story of Sodom and Gomorrah. Yahweh gets angry at a town for their promiscuous ways so he sends down fire and destruction. Lot and his family are saved until his wife turns to look at the physical manifestation of Yahweh's wrath. The Christian deity gets angry at her for her disobedience and transforms her into a pillar of salt. Unfortunately, most have not actually read the full story from their Bibles. Most are not familiar with the details of this disturbing, incestuous story.

It all starts in Genesis 18 when one day, unable to see things from his cloud, Yahweh tells his human friend, Abraham, that he "will go down" to Sodom to "see if what they" had "done" was "as bad as the outcry that" had "reached" him (Genesis 18:21). How long does it take an outcry to reach the Christian deity? The Israelites were enslaved for over "four hundred years" before Yahweh "heard them crying out" (Acts 7:6) (Exodus 3:7). Again, the Bible fails to give us the needed information and because of this, we may never know how long these particular cries where circulating before Yahweh finally noticed them.

Now Lot, the nephew of Yahweh's friend Abraham, lived in Sodom with his family. This complicated things a bit. Yahweh's plan was to destroy the sinful city. Yet, the Christian deity found this man "Lot" to be "a righteous man" with a "righteous soul" and, therefore, worthy of being saved (2 Peter 2:7,8). He had promised Abraham he would not "sweep away the righteous with the wicked" (Genesis 18:23). Since the concept of a protective force field had not yet been thought up, Yahweh decided he physically needed to go down to Sodom and bring out Lot's family before he destroyed the city.

Yahweh did not end up going on his trip to Sodom. Instead, he sent down a pair of his male angels to investigate something he should have already known. When Yahweh's angel men arrived at

Lot's residence, a crowd formed and "surrounded the house" (Genesis 19:4). The mob consisted entirely of "men from every part of the city...both young and old" (Genesis 19:4). They demanded that Lot bring out his two male visitors so that they could "have sex with them" (Genesis 19:5). Lot would not stand for such a "wicked thing" (Genesis 19:7). He went outside to talk some sense into these wild men.

"Look," Lot told them, "I have two daughters who have never slept with a man. Let me bring them out to you, and you can do what you like with them" (Genesis 19:8). Lot, the man Yahweh felt was righteous enough to save, did not hesitate to throw his own children out into the night to be raped by an entire city of men. His daughters were nothing more than expendable property to him, disposable possessions, bargaining chips. Lot even attempted to sweeten the deal by disclosing his daughter's virginity. Fresh meat, never touched.

Lot would have allowed the mob to do anything they wanted to his daughters, but to his visitors, he told them not to "do anything...for they" were "under the protection of" his "roof" (Genesis 19:8). His own children were not under the protection of his roof. They were not safe from their righteous father's readiness to throw them out to a mob of horny men to be sexually assaulted as a substitute for his attractive visitors. How many Christians would do as Lot did? How many would be so quick and eager to offer up their own daughters to an aroused crowd? Would you consider someone who is so willing to throw his own virgin daughters out to be raped a righteous man?

After the Christian deity "struck the men...with blindness," Lot and his family were able to escape the barrage of men and flee the city (Genesis 19:11). While Yahweh was destroying the city, Lot and his family were told not to "stop anywhere" or "look back" at the destruction (Genesis 19:17). They were told to "flee to the mountains or...be swept away" (Genesis 19:17). "But Lot's wife" (who does not get a name) "looked back, and" immediately Yahweh turned her into "a pillar of salt" for her failure to follow his ridiculous rule (Genesis 19:26).

Lot and his two daughters headed to "the mountains" and took up residence "in a cave" (Genesis 19:30). "One day" Lot's "older daughter" began to voice her fears concerning the preservation of the "family line" to her younger sister (Genesis 19:31-32). She believed there was "no man around" to impregnate them (Genesis 19:31). Her solution was to get their "father to drink" a bunch of "wine and then sleep with him" (Genesis 19:31-33). "That night they got their father to drink wine, and the older daughter went in and slept with him" (Genesis 19:33). The Bible tells us that Lot "was not aware" of his daughter's incestuous act (Genesis 19:33). The next night, "they got their father to drink wine" again, and this time "the younger daughter went in and slept with him" (Genesis 19:35). We are told that Lot "was not aware" of his youngest daughter's incestuous act either (Genesis 19:35). In the end, "both of Lot's daughters became pregnant by their father" (Genesis 19:36).

Millions of people around the world believe their children should pick up a Bible and read it every day, unfiltered and unsupervised. How is this suitable for all ages? Why would anyone want their child to read this garbage? This is one of the many reasons why I strongly believe there should be a parental advisory label placed on every Bible.

In the book of Judges, we find the story of a man who does not come with a formal name but is instead only referred to as "a Levite" (Judges 19:1). This "Levite" had himself a "concubine" that "was unfaithful to him...and went back to her parents' home" (Judges 19:1-2). After the Levite retrieved his lost property from her father's place, they "left and went toward" the Levite's home (Judges 19:10). They would not reach their destination before nightfall, so he decided to stop and "spend the night in" a town called "Gibeah" (Judges 19:13). When the Levite reached "Gibeah...an old man" came to him in the square and welcomed him and his concubine into his home for the night (Judges 19:16). Just as "the old man" and the Levite had begun "enjoying themselves, some of the wicked men of the city surrounded the house" (Judges 19:22). The mob started "pounding on the door," demanding that "the old man...bring out the" Levite so that they may "have sex with him" (Judges 19:22).

The old man "went outside" to try to talk the mob down (Judges 19:23). "Don't be so vile," he told them, "don't do this outrageous thing" (Judges 19:23). "Look," said the old man, "here is my virgin daughter, and" the Levite's "concubine. I will bring them out to you now, and you can use them and do whatever you wish" (Judges 19:24). This old man sounds just like Lot. The similarities are uncanny. In the book of Genesis, Lot tells the men of Sodom that he has "two daughters who have never slept with a man" and to "let" him "bring them out to" the men, so that they could "do what" they "like with" his daughters (Genesis 19:8). Both men, Lot and the old man described in the book of Judges, without hesitation, offered to throw their own daughters out to be raped by an entire town.

Both of the men scolded the crowd for wanting to do such a disgraceful thing to their guests. But to their own daughters, to their own children, without any remorse or reluctance, they would allow the crowd to "do what" they "like" (Genesis 19:8). According to the Bible, Yahweh's own breathed out words, it is more disgraceful and vile for a group of men to want to commit sexual acts on another man than it is to give one's virgin daughters up to be raped by a horde of violently horny townsmen. The Christian "Good Book" contains stories in which women are treated as dispensable fleshy property without rebuttal.

After the old man failed to calm the crowd, the Levite made a rash decision. He "took his concubine," like she was a dog that had just soiled the rug and tossed "her outside to them" (Judges 19:25). The men of the town "raped her and abused her throughout the night" (Judges 19:25). When dawn broke, and the men had their fill, she crawled back to the house and "fell down at the door" and died (Judges 19:26). "In the morning," the Levite discovered her broken body lying "in the doorway" (Judges 19:27). He told his concubine to "get up," continuing with, "let's go" (Judges 19:28). No sympathy was shown toward her, no remorse for his actions.

There are many similarities between the Levite story and the one of Lot. Yahweh has stated previously that everything in the Bible "is useful for teaching, rebuking, correcting and training in righteousness" (2 Timothy 3:16). The Christian deity felt it necessary and important enough to tell us twice that one's daughters can be used as fleshy fodder to protect one's guests. Is that the purpose of this appalling storyline? Is this the message he is attempting to convey to the world?

The Christian deity hindered the freedoms of women, and he reduced them to a lower class of being. In his churches, "women…are not allowed to speak" because he wants them to learn in full "submission" (1 Corinthians 14:34). Yahweh finds it "disgraceful for a woman to" even talk while in his churches (1 Corinthians 14:35). If they have a question, Yahweh wants them to wait and go "ask their own husbands at home" (1 Corinthians 14:35). Adding to his sexist gag order, Yahweh declares in the book of 1 Timothy that "a woman should learn in quietness and full submission" (1 Timothy 2:11). Women "must be quiet" in his church (1 Timothy 2:12). This is his rule, his perfect law. Yahweh wants women to be silenced and kept from bothering his favorite people, men.

The Christian deity clearly feels that women are not equal to men. Why does he want us to see women this way? What did they do to deserve such sexist treatment from a loving, perfect being? According to the book of 1 Timothy, the Christian deity believes that because "Adam was formed" before "Eve," and because he believes "Adam was not the one deceived," and that "it was the woman who was deceived and became a sinner," he can add things to his book that are degrading to women and promote them as expendable commodities (1 Timothy 2:13-14). The Bible blames Eve.

Why does Yahweh only blame the woman? Was Adam not deceived as well? Both of them were deceived by Yahweh. The serpent told Adam and Eve the truth about the fruit on the tree, saying that "when you eat from it your eyes will be opened, and you will be like God, knowing good and evil" (Genesis 3:5). Yahweh told them that if they even "touch" the "fruit," they would "die" (Genesis 3:3). Adam and Eve both partook of the forbidden fruit and realized that they did indeed not die, but instead, gained the knowledge of good and evil, right from wrong, just like the serpent had said. Yahweh had deceived them both. And even if you think the serpent did the deceiving, Adam was right there alongside his counterpart listening to the serpent and eating the fruit. Meaning, no matter how you look at it, they were both deceived, both man and woman.

The misogynistic ideals found inside the Bible are disadvantageous to women. As an all-knowing being, Yahweh was aware of the difficulties women would go through because of the words he put forth, because of the archaic and ignorant rules he personally installed. Why would he purposefully hinder the advancement of equal rights? Why would he not do a better job of protecting women? He clearly does not have their best interests in mind.

What if the guy dating your daughter demanded she apologize to him every time she had her period? What if he required her to be silent while she was in his house? Would you want your daughter dating this guy? Would you not feel he was mistreating your little girl? Most of the Christians I know would never allow their daughters to date someone who treats women this way. Why then do they want their daughters to have a personal relationship with a deity that demands the same things? Why does Yahweh get a pass? Why does his misogynistic world view get overlooked and or shrugged off as no big deal? Why would anyone want to worship such a monster!?

Chapter 6

Basic Instructions Before Leaving Earth

To the majority of Christians, the Bible is their ultimate source of moralistic guidance. They believe it was given to them by their creator deity to use as a manual, a tool useful for "teaching, rebuking, correcting and training" (2 Timothy 3:16). Inside this holy handbook, 613 laws teach us just how the Christian deity expects things to be done. Utterly convinced of his own superiority, Yahweh considers his set of rules to be "perfect" (Psalm 19:7) and "holy, righteous and good" (Romans 7:12).

Jesus referenced the Old Testament and the laws given within on several occasions. Quoting from Deuteronomy, Jesus indicates that "man does not live by bread alone but on every word that comes from the mouth of" Yahweh (Deuteronomy 8:3). Jesus does not say to live by every word, except for the laws provided in the Old Testament. According to 2 Timothy 3:16, all 613 of these laws came from the mouth of Yahweh. Jesus is clearly lumping in the laws when he says to follow every word that comes from Yahweh's mouth.

When Jesus spoke of the Old Testament laws, he portrayed them as something that was still relevant, still to be upheld and followed. He claimed "it is easier for heaven and earth to disappear than" it is "for the least stroke of a pen to drop out of the law" (Luke 16:17). He taught that "until heaven and earth disappear, not the smallest letter, not the least stroke of a pen, will by any means disappear from the law" (Matthew 5:18). According to Revelation 21, "heaven" and "earth" will not be destroyed, will not disappear, until Yahweh's pointless drama has played out (Revelation 21:1). Meaning, the Christian deity, still finds his laws to be applicable, he still wants them to be observed today.

Jesus taught that "anyone who" breaks "one of the least of these commands and teaches others accordingly will be called least in the kingdom of heaven, but whoever practices and teaches these commands will be called great in...heaven" (Matthew 5:19). No self-respecting Christian wants to be called least when they reach their eternal home. Most would love nothing more than to be called great by their creator deity. If a Christian wants to avoid being considered a lower class of heavenly people, if they are looking to get that status bump when they get to the happiest place off earth, they should follow the rules Yahweh has put in place. The rules he deems to be perfect.

Using his Yahweh-given authority, Jesus expanded on his father's divorce laws previously established in Deuteronomy 24. He changed the act of divorce and the remarrying of divorced women into a crime punishable by death. The Christian demigod informed his followers that "anyone who divorces his wife" for any reason other than "for sexual immorality, makes her" an adulteress (Matthew 5:32). He goes on to say that "anyone who marries a divorced woman" also "commits adultery" (Matthew 5:32). Way back in the Old Testament, Yahweh made the rule that people who commit "adultery," must "be put to death" (Leviticus 20:10). The Christian demigod is advocating for the death of divorcees. This is the law Jesus says to follow. These are the rules set forth by the perfect Christian deities.

Jesus not only promoted the laws his father put in place but scolded those that chose to ignore them. One day, while "Jesus" was out having dinner with his friends, the "teachers of the law" confronted them for not following "tradition" (Matthew 15:1-2).

"Jesus," having none of this, turned it around and scolded them for not following a "command of" Yahweh (Matthew 15:3). He reminded these teachers that Yahweh had commanded us all to "honor" our "father and mother, and" that "anyone who curses their father or mother is to be put to death" (Matthew 15:4). Jesus calls them "hypocrites" for not following this holy rule (Matthew 15:7). The Christian poster boy for love and kindness is advocating for the death of rebellious children. This story is repeated, with minor differences in Mark 7:9-10.

It is in the book of Leviticus that Yahweh permanently installs the rule declaring "death" for "anyone who curses their father or mother" (Leviticus 20:9). The Christian deity finds it just and fair to throw rocks at a disrespectful child until they die. Yahweh not only condones the killing of children, but he calls for it, he demands it. If this was actually a law Christians followed, there would probably be a shortage of teenagers in the world. Cursing at or wishing curses upon one's parents is a crime punishable by death in Yahweh's mind.

In addition to unruly children, the Christian deity wants his followers to murder magical people. If "a medium or spiritist" is found "among" his people, Yahweh wants them to be stoned "to death" (Leviticus 20:27). They are "not" to "allow a sorceress to live" (Exodus 22:18). The Christian deity believes that people are doing real magic and that they should all be destroyed for doing it. Why are Christians not on the streets searching for witches to vanquish? Why do they not kill when their loving deity tells them to?

Yahweh wants his people to murder anyone who dares to "do any work" on his holy day of rest (Exodus 20:10). One time a group of Yahweh's favorite people discovered "a man...gathering wood on the Sabbath day" (Numbers 15:32). They "brought" the lawbreaker "to Moses and Aaron and the whole assembly, and they kept him in custody" (Numbers 15:33-34). The loving Christian deity decided not to show any mercy. He informed his people that "the man must die" for his offensive stick gathering (Numbers 15:35). Yahweh's appalling orders were carried out, the whole "assembly took him outside of the camp and stoned him to death" (Numbers 15:36).

Yahweh implemented the death penalty for a variety of silly reasons. "Do not let your hair become unkempt...or you will die, and" Yahweh will become "angry with the whole community" (Leviticus 10:6). "Drink wine" before entering his special "tent of meeting" and "you will die" (Leviticus 10:9). If you "leave the entrance to the tent of meeting" with Yahweh's special "oil...on you," the Bible says "you will die" (Leviticus 10:7). "Whoever touches the mountain" while Yahweh is on it "is to be put to death" by being "stoned or shot with arrows" (Exodus 19:12-13). How are these irrational rules and their excessive punishments found to be justifiable? How can anyone find this deity worthy of praise and worship?

Yahweh's grotesque set of laws have been used to promote some of the most egregious acts in human history. Countless have suffered and died on account of Yahweh's calling for "slaves" to "obey" their "earthly masters with respect and fear...just as" they "would obey Christ" (Ephesians 6:5). The deity Christians worship commanded that slave masters be feared as Jesus is feared, to be obeyed as Jesus is to be obeyed. Yahweh gave slave masters ultimate power over the people they owned. He did this knowing the consequences of his actions, knowing the death and pain it would cause. Yahweh, the loving Christian deity, thought this was a flawless rule.

This icon of perfection not only condones the owning of people as property but the abuse from their masters as well. The Christian deity believes that "anyone who beats their male or female slave with a rod must be punished if the slave dies as a direct result, but they are not to be punished if the slave recovers after a day or two" (Exodus 21:20). The perfect Christian deity wanted his people to know that it is entirely acceptable to beat their slaves "since the slave is their property" (Exodus 21:21). Yahweh believes "slaves" should "submit" themselves to their "masters" even "to those who are harsh" (1 Peter 2:18). Yahweh finds it "commendable" to endure "unjust suffering" (1 Peter 2:19).

In the book of Exodus, Yahweh shows us how to regulate the sale of one's own "daughter as a servant" (Exodus 21:7). The Christian deity believes that "if a man sells his daughter as a servant," then "she is not to go free as male servants do" (Exodus 21:7). The almighty good guy in the sky condones and regulates the selling of children. Going through some tough times? Having trouble feeding that fourth kid? Instead of keeping his promise to not "let the righteous go hungry," instead of providing a little extra food for those in need, the Christian deity recommends you sell off your kids as servants (Proverbs 10:3).

Yahweh, the source of all Christian morality fails to mention that slavery should be abolished and condemned. The Christian deity has no objections to people being sold as property. According to the Bible, he supports and regulates it. Yahweh even gives the slave masters authority equal to that of the Christian demigod himself. Most of the Christians I have encountered believe Yahweh is against slavery. Where does this blatantly fallacious concept come from?

The Christian creator deity wants his followers to "keep his requirements, his decrees, his laws and his commands always" (Deuteronomy 11:1). Nowhere does it say to stop following the laws of Yahweh. Most Christians want to do everything they can to please their heavenly father figure. Yet when he tells them to "keep his commands and obey him," they fail (Deuteronomy 13:4). If all of these laws were thought up and put in place by the Christian deity himself, why then do Christians try and distance themselves from the majority of them? Why does every Christian politician shy away from implementing these perfect Yahweh-endorsed laws and regulations?

When you ask a Christian which laws they are supposed to be following, most of them will tell you the Ten Commandments. Yet nowhere in the Bible does it say only to follow the Ten Commandments. They have to pick and choose which verses they like and which ones do not fit their personal view of Christianity. My mother always told me that people who pick and choose their Bible verses to follow are called scissors Christians. I have come to the realization that, in fact, they are all scissors Christians. They cannot follow the laws of Yahweh and live in a civilized society.

When a Christian is unable to obey the rules their deity put in place, when Yahweh says to do something they feel is morally reprehensible, they have to come up with excuses, or apologetics. Christians must distance themselves from a set of commands that have no place in the modern world. Using the book of Romans, most Christians will claim that Jesus was "the culmination," or end, "of the law" (Romans 10:4). Although this statement is a blatant contradiction, it is still biblically accurate. In the book of Romans, Paul is saying there is no more law. However, this is not what Jesus taught, and this is not what Yahweh commanded. This is merely an excuse to get out of the substantial amount of killing they would have to do on a daily basis if they followed the orders of their eccentric deity.

Even if we choose to believe that Yahweh no longer requires the death of those who pick up sticks on the Sabbath because of Jesus, the issue still remains; at one point, he thought it was a great idea. There was a time when the deity Christians worship thought it was morally acceptable to own people as property and to throw rocks at disobedient children until they die. These are the things he finds to be holy, righteous, and good.

What about heaven? Do Christians actually think Yahweh's house will be void of Yahweh's perfect rules? Could you imagine an eternity without eating "pig" (Leviticus 11:7)? No more bacon. No more pulled pork sandwiches. Why would anyone look forward to such a nightmare!? Why would anyone want to worship such a monster!?

Chapter 7

For Yahweh so Loved Himself

Through his own breathed out words, the Christian deity expresses his disdain for those who are prideful or "conceited" (Romans 12:16). The Bible says that Yahweh "detests all the proud of heart" and that he will not allow those who think too highly of themselves to "go unpunished" (Proverbs 16:5). He "opposes the proud" (1 Peter 5:5). He teaches that "pride goes before destruction" and that a prideful "spirit" comes "before a fall" (Proverbs 16:18). Yahweh holds so much "hate" toward "pride and arrogance" (Proverbs 8:13) that he once turned a conceited king into a strange "bird" creature that "ate grass" (Daniel 4:33).

In the book of Daniel, we find the story of King Nebuchadnezzar, whose inflated ego did not go unnoticed. Instead of seeking to glorify Yahweh, he sought "glory" for himself and boasted about his "mighty power" (Daniel 4:30). The Christian deity decided to punish King Nebuchadnezzar for having an ego. Using magical "dew from heaven," Yahweh transformed him into a "grass" eating creature with "feathers of an eagle" and "nails like the claws of a bird" (Daniel 4:33). Yahweh forced this man to live as an animal until he raised his "eyes toward heaven and praised" him (Daniel 4:34). Yahweh needed to teach this man a lesson, he needed him to pay for thinking too highly of himself.

The Christian deity frowns upon those who are proud and self-centered. Yet, we find throughout the Bible Yahweh demanding attention and bragging about how awesome he is. He believes that "no one can" even "fathom" "his greatness," that he alone is "great" and "worthy of praise" (Psalm 145:3). Yahweh wants his "name" to "be proclaimed in all the earth" (Exodus 9:16). He wants "incense and pure offerings...brought to" him (Malachi 1:11). He even wants us all to "sing" praises to his "name" (Psalm 61:8). How is this not seen as prideful and arrogant? Why does Yahweh get a pass? Is it not sinful when the creator sins?

The Bible says that the very "name of" Yahweh holds such importance that one must never "misuse" it (Deuteronomy 5:11). The loving Christian deity wants "anyone who blasphemes" his "name...to be put to death" (Leviticus 24:16). Yahweh truly despises bad press. No second chances, one slip of the tongue, and he wants you to pay for it with your life. What could be so special about a name that its cursing comes with a death sentence?

The Christian deity finds himself to be so important that he decided to make a special day all about him. After Yahweh spent "six days" creating the world, he "rested on the seventh day," and "blessed" what he called "the Sabbath day and made it holy" (Exodus 20:11). Because he took this time off, Yahweh now requires us all to "remember" this "day" by "not" doing "any work" (Exodus 20:8-10). This is not a request, it is a perfect policy that must be followed and obeyed, or the Christian deity will have you killed. He wants those who dare work on his holy day of rest to be "stoned...to death" (Numbers 15:36).

Yahweh finds himself to be the most superior deity among all the other deities worshiped by people. He is so adamant about his own supremacy that he demands to be the only one worshiped: "you shall have no other gods before me" (Deuteronomy 5:7). He needs the attention; he thrives off of it. He gets jealous and violent when attention is given to another. No one is allowed to "bow down to...or worship" figurines in the form of other deities or the "jealous God" Christians worship will punish "children for the sin of" their "parents" up "to the third and fourth generation" (Exodus 20:5). He needs to be the only one you worship; he requires complete loyalty. Only give attention to the Christian deity, or he will punish the children in your family for generations to come.

Yahweh wants "those who have" joined in worshiping "Baal" to be "put to death" (Numbers 25:5). He wants those who have killed animals "to any god other than" him to "be destroyed" (Exodus 22:20). He calls for the death of those who invite others to worship a different deity. "If your very own brother, or your son or daughter, or the wife you love," not the other one, "or your closest friend secretly entices you, saying, 'Let us go and worship other gods,'" Yahweh wants you to "show them no pity," commanding that you "do not spare them" and that "you must certainly put them to death" (Deuteronomy 13:6-9). Yahweh wants you to "stone them to death, because they tried to turn you away from" him (Deuteronomy 13:10). Worship or sacrifice to someone else and the temperamental Christian deity will have you killed.

Yahweh does not want anyone he feels has a "defect" to be anywhere "near" his "curtain or" his "altar" (Leviticus 21:23). "No man who is blind or lame, disfigured or deformed; no man with a crippled foot or hand, or who is a hunchback or dwarf, or who has an eye defect...or damaged testicles" will be allowed in his holy place, touching his holy stuff (Leviticus 21:18-20). Yahweh believes these people have the power to "desecrate" his "sanctuary" (Leviticus 21:23). What makes Yahweh's stuff so special that not even a man with crushed testicles is allowed to go near it? Why is he so petty?

Have you ever wondered what Yahweh's throne must look like? A deity who thinks this highly of himself must have an impressive throne from which to rule. Encircled by "a rainbow" and capable of producing "flashes of lightning" with "rumblings and peals of thunder," the Christian deity sits upon a "throne" of his own creation (Revelation 4:3-5). "Surrounding the throne" Yahweh built, there are "twenty-four other thrones" with "twenty-four elders" sitting on them (Revelation 4:4). "Four living creatures" with "six wings" and "eyes all around, even under" their "wings," sit "in the center, around the throne" all "day and night" repeating: "Holy, holy, holy is the Lord God Almighty, who was, and is, and is to come" (Revelation 4:6-8). "Whenever the living creatures" covered in eyeballs "give glory and honor to" Yahweh, "the twenty-four elders fall down before him" and "worship him" (Revelation 4:9-10). "They lay their crowns before" Yahweh and tell him that he is "worthy" to "receive glory and honor and power" because he "created all things" (Revelation 4:10-11). Yahweh wants to be glorified so badly that he creates beings whose sole purpose in life is to spout out praises to him all day and all night, "never" stopping (Revelation 4:8). If you had the powers of creation, as Yahweh does in his stories, would you construct beings to fly around all day and night, saying how awesome you are? Would you demand attention and gratification for all of your accomplishments?

Yahweh expects "praise and honor and glory and power, for ever and ever" (Revelation 5:13). He requires recognition, he demands to be loved and respected. He wants us to "fear" him, "praise him...honor him," and "revere him" (Psalm 22:23). He wants "the wild animals" to "honor" him (Isaiah 43:20). The self-centered Christian deity wants "every creature" to "praise" him "for ever and ever (Psalm 145:21). If you do not do these things, "if you do not listen" to him and you "do not...honor" him, then he "will send a curse on you" (Malachi 2:2). "If anyone does not love" Yahweh, he wants them to "be cursed" (1 Corinthians 16:22).

Imagine if you will, a man who has created a terminal disease capable of causing massive amounts of pain and suffering. Along with this harmful creation, the man makes an antidote, a cure. He then takes his debilitating disease and spreads it throughout the entire world, infecting every human being on the planet. How would you feel about him if he chose to only allow those who love him and are willing to bow down and worship him access to his cure? If you do not love and praise this man, then he will watch you suffer and die. Do these sound like the actions of a loving being? Would you find this man worthy of praise?

The Christian deity has done this exact thing. He has created a disease—sin—and then offered the cure—the blood of his son, the demigod. Before you can receive this cure, he requires you to worship and adore him. If you do not, he will send you to his personal torture chamber for eternity. Honor me or die. Love me or burn. These are the demands of the deity Christians worship. These are his conditions. What kind of self-absorbed madman demands worship and recognition for offering a cure to a disease that he created on purpose? Why would anyone want to worship such an egotistical monster?

Chapter 8

Free Will be Damned

Before we can discuss free will, we must first define it. According to dictionary.com, free will is "the power of making free choices unconstrained by external agencies." The Encyclopedia Britannica states that free will is "the power or capacity...to act in certain situations independently of natural, social, or divine restraints." Most Christians maintain the belief that we all get free will. This belief, however, is not biblically accurate. The Bible never claims we all get free will, not one verse. The Christian deity will manipulate a situation, interfere, and even threaten his creations into submission. Yahweh "does whatever pleases him" (Psalm 115:3).

Most Christians will often refer to the story of creation in Genesis 2-3 as an example of free will. They believe that because Adam and Eve were able to choose whether or not to eat from Yahweh's magical tree, we all get free will. Adam and Eve were not free from the influence of an outside source. Yahweh stepped in and planted his deadly fruit trees in the center of his perfect garden. He could have stored these trees literally anywhere else. Still, he chose to put them in the path of his creations, forever altering humanity. Yahweh further influenced their decision by packaging death in the shape of a safe and familiar object. The Christian deity chose to use magical fruit to set mankind on an endless journey seeking redemption from him. This was all part of his perfect plan. With the tree planted right "in the middle of the garden," the trap was set (Genesis 2:9). All he had to do was wait for the serpent to do the job he designed him to do. This is not an example of free will.

When Adam and Eve ate the forbidden fruit, they did not die as the Christian deity had eluded to in Genesis, when he stated that if they "eat from the tree of the knowledge of good and evil" they "will certainly die" (Genesis 2:17). They certainly did not die when they ate it. Which means Yahweh either lied about the consequences of touching his magical tree or he failed to know what would happen if his humans interacted with it. Instead of death, Adam and Eve gained the knowledge of good and evil. They were able to understand right from wrong. This means that Adam and Eve did not start off knowing right from wrong; they did not have the knowledge of good and evil. The all-knowing Christian deity chose to store a tree with the potential to cause the fall of man in a garden where he kept a pair of humans with the moral capacity of a toddler.

Suppose someone placed a gummy bear filled with rat poison in the middle of a daycare. What if they then told every kid in the room not to touch it or they would die and then left the room? What if after leaving the room this person allowed a crafty stranger into the daycare to try and convince the children to eat the poisoned treat? How long before one of those kids grabs the deadly gummy and eats it? Without the placement of the harmful object and the introduction of an antagonist poised to influence them to do the wrong thing, there would be no dead child, there would be no fall of man.

Who is to blame for the death of the toddler that ingested the poison? It is not the fault of the child. They did not fully understand right from wrong. Once the poison was introduced, once the fruit tree was placed, the toddlers in the room became victims. The one who put the poison in an otherwise safe environment is to blame.

Why did Yahweh start human beings off without the knowledge of good and evil? Why would he make it an extra ability that is forbidden to have and then dangle it in their faces? He teased the possibility of them being able to mature in their understanding of the world around them, about life itself. Yahweh created mankind with a thirst for knowledge and yet made that knowledge a damnable offense.

Furthermore, why would Yahweh make a tree with fruit that magically gives the consumer the ability to know right from wrong in the first place? What purpose would it serve an all-knowing deity? He should already possess the knowledge contained in the fruit. Other than needing it to tempt his childlike creations, why would he choose to make such a tree?

In the book of Habakkuk, we find Yahweh engaged in a conversation with one of his prophets. The prophet Habakkuk cried "out to" Yahweh inquiring, "how long...must" he "call for help" (Habakkuk 1:2). He had been crying out to Yahweh, "Violence!" and yet Yahweh did "not save" him (Habakkuk 1:2). Habakkuk wanted to know why his deity was ignoring all the "destruction and violence," and asked "why" Yahweh would "tolerate" all the "wrongdoing" (Habakkuk 1:3). Yahweh explained to his prophet, the reason things had gotten so bad was that he was personally "rising up," a group of "ruthless and impetuous people" called "the Babylonians" (Habakkuk 1:6). The Bible says the Babylonian "hordes" were bent on violence, and advanced "like a desert wind" (Habakkuk 1:9). These people did not rise up on their own. The loving Christian deity interfered in the lives of humans by raising up ruthless people to attack them. This was all part of Yahweh's perfect plan. This is not an example of free will.

Before the Old Testament hero, David, was king of Israel, a man named Saul occupied the position. According to 1 Samuel, during this time, "David" would play a small harp while his king "was prophesying in his house" (1 Samuel 18:10). One "day an evil spirit from" Yahweh "came forcefully on Saul" (1 Samuel 18:10). The possessed king cried out, "I'll pin David to the wall" (1 Samuel 18:11). "Saul" simultaneously "hurled" the "spear in his hand" at David (1 Samuel 18:10-11). "Twice," the mad king threw his spear, missing the target (1 Samuel 18:11). David managed to dodge both throws and escape without a scratch.

Despite barely escaping with his life, the Bible says David eventually went back to "playing the harp" for his king (1 Samuel 19:9). One day, while "Saul" "was sitting in his house" listening to David play, Yahweh sent another "evil spirit" down to possess the king (1 Samuel 19:9). Just as before, while under the influence of this evil spirit, "Saul tried to pin" David against "the wall with his spear" (1 Samuel 19:10). "David eluded him" and escaped once more (1 Samuel 19:10).

Saul did not hurl these spears at David on his own. His hand was forced by an evil outside influence sent by the Christian deity. For reasons untold, Yahweh wanted to possess a man with a malicious ghost causing him to become pointlessly violent. This is something the loving Christian deity chose to do.

In the book of 2 Thessalonians, Yahweh sent an unspecified amount of people "a powerful delusion so that they" would "believe" a "lie" (2 Thessalonians 2:11). He did this because he believed they were "perishing" due to their refusal "to love the truth and so be saved" (2 Thessalonians 2:10). Once Yahweh had deceived the "perishing" people, once he personally caused them to believe a lie, he "condemned" them for it (2 Thessalonians 2:10-12). Yahweh confessed to deliberately tricking people into believing a fatal falsehood. He knew his deception would be the cause of their demise. He wanted it this way. He set these things in motion on purpose so that his will for them could be accomplished: "give thanks in all circumstances; for this is God's will for you" (1 Thessalonians 5:18).

In Exodus, the Christian deity prevents the pharaoh from listening and complying with his demands. Did the pharaoh have a choice when Yahweh hardened his heart in Exodus 9:12, 10:20, 10:27, 11:10, and 14:8? The Christian deity forced the pharaoh to deny the release of the Israelite people, provoking him to send forth death and destruction in the form of ten plagues. During the last plague, the loving Christian deity "struck down all the firstborn in Egypt" (Exodus 12:29). Yahweh claims to have done all of this to show off his "power" and have his "name…proclaimed in all the earth" (Romans 9:17). The Christian deity admits that he "will gain glory for" himself "through Pharaoh and his army" (Exodus 14:4). Yahweh "raised" Pharaoh "up for this very purpose" (Romans 9:17). He "has mercy on whom he wants to have mercy, and he hardens whom he wants to harden" (Romans 9:18). This is not free will.

Does Yahweh allow his people free will in heaven? If they have free will in heaven, then they can sin in heaven, which means heaven is not a perfect place. If there is no free will in heaven, then they are all forced to do whatever this deity wants for eternity, and heaven is not a perfect place. Yahweh addresses this issue in Revelation, where he admits that "his servants," Christians who are now living in heaven, "will serve him" and "his name will be on their foreheads" for eternity (Revelation 22:3-4). Christians are not going to be given a choice. This is all part of the plan. They are in heaven to serve their deity without question. Why does an all-powerful, loving being desire to have servants? If you are under the service of someone else, you are not free. This is not an example free will.

The Bible says that "in their hearts, humans plan their course, but" Yahweh "establishes their steps" (Proverbs 16:9). Free will be damned. Yahweh "is in heaven; he does whatever pleases him" (Psalm 115:3). He will meddle with the hearts and thoughts of his creations in order to implement his will. "He does as he pleases with the powers of heaven and the peoples of the earth" (Daniel 4:35). "No one can hold back his hand or say to him: 'What have you done?'" (Daniel 4:35). Yahweh's "dominion is an eternal dominion" and "all the peoples of the earth are regarded as nothing" (Daniel 4:34-35). Why would anyone want to worship such a monster?

Chapter 9

Eternal Housing

Most Christians believe that once our flesh dies off, an invisible part of us called a soul will leave our bodies and live on forever. Their entire lives are based on this premise, this unfounded hope of an afterlife. Needing a place to store these eternal human leftovers, the Christian deity constructed two unique locations in which to keep them. Yahweh calls his permanent housing heaven and hell. One he created for eternal punishment and the other for perpetual servitude. Each built and controlled by the Christian deity himself. He sets the rules and determines who gets to go to which afterlife location based on their loyalty to him.

Yahweh "prepared a city for" those he deemed worthy of his presence (Hebrews 11:16). He called this "Holy City the new Jerusalem," Revelation describes it "as a bride beautifully dressed for her husband" (Revelation 21:2). "The foundations of the city walls" are "decorated with every kind of precious stone" (Revelation 21:19). The walls themselves are "made of jasper, and the city of pure gold" (Revelation 21:18). Each of "the twelve gates" in heaven are "made of a single pearl," and the main "street" is made "of gold, as pure as transparent glass" (Revelation 21:21). Heaven, Yahweh's infamous city in the sky, according to the Bible, is nothing more than a flashier, upgraded version of Yahweh's favorite city in the whole wide world, Jerusalem.

Why does the Christian deity need walls covered with precious stones and his entire city made out of pure gold? Why is there such a grotesque display of wealth in Yahweh's upgraded city? Why is he so flashy? Does he think that it makes his city or even himself look better or more important? The Christian deity might prefer his architecture to be shiny and bedazzled, but some people might find his decorating style and abundant use of the color gold a bit over the top for their taste.

Yahweh's new Jerusalem will come complete with "high" walls and "twelve gates" guarded by "twelve angels" (Revelation 21:12). Why did the Christian deity build a wall around heaven? Yahweh tells us that in his heaven, "thieves do not break in and steal" (Matthew 6:20). Why then does he need a wall with guarded gates? Did Yahweh build his walls for a more sinister purpose? What if the walls are there to keep souls from escaping Yahweh's perfect golden city? What happens in heaven? What do the servants of Yahweh do all day? How do they pass the time, card games, shuffleboard? Is there shuffleboard in heaven?

The Bible says that in heaven, Christians will be "servants" to their loving deity "for ever and ever" (Revelation 22:3,5). He will write his "name" onto "their foreheads," marking his property like the slave masters of old (Revelation 22:4). This is Yahweh's perfect plan for his followers, eternal subjugation. As an all-powerful being, he is more than capable of serving himself. Why does the Christian deity desire to be served, and why are Christians so excited to do it? Naturally, some of these slaves would tire of serving their self-centered deity all day every day and want to escape the control he has over them. That must be where the walls with gates and guards come in.

Yahweh, claims that his "city does not need the sun or the moon to shine on it" (Revelation 21:23) Why? Because he believes he radiates so much honor and grandeur that he acts as a "light" source for everybody in the city (Revelation 21:23). Yahweh's narcissistic glow never turns off, meaning "there will be no night" in heaven (Revelation 21:25). Why would that be a good thing? In heaven, you will never again watch the beauty of a rising and setting sun or enjoy another night spent underneath the stars. Yahweh's golden cage does not have such things.

In the book of Matthew, the Christian demigod talks about how he "will separate the people one from another as a shepherd separates the sheep from the goats" (Matthew 25:32). "He will put the sheep on his right and the goats on his left" (Matthew 25:33). The sheep, Yahweh explains, have a golden "kingdom prepared for" them, an "inheritance" waiting as compensation for being such obedient followers (Matthew 25:34). Yahweh wants the goats, the creatures on his left, to "depart from" him "into the eternal fire prepared for the devil and his angels" (Matthew 25:41). Since these goats failed to feed "hungry" people, "clothe" the poor, or give those who are "thirsty" something to drink, Yahweh wants them to "go away to eternal punishment" (Matthew 25:42-46). If you do not do what the loving Christian deity tells you to do, he will send you to hell to be tortured forever.

Yahweh regulates the population of each eternal realm, and he personally directs the inflow of human traffic. Like Santa Claus checking his list of naughty and nice children, Yahweh checks his special book to see who qualifies to serve him forever in a place he refers to as "paradise" (Luke 23:43). The Bible says Yahweh will judge our souls "for the things done while in the body, whether good or bad" (2 Corinthians 5:10). When you do the things he likes, he puts your name in the book of life. But if the Christian deity cannot locate your name in his special "book," then you will be "thrown into the lake of fire" forever (Revelation 20:15).

Yahweh wants "the cowardly, the "unbelieving...and all liars" to be placed into the eternal "fiery lake of burning sulfur" (Revelation 21:8). "He will punish those who do not know" him "and do not obey the gospel" with an "everlasting destruction" (2 Thessalonians 1:8-9). Perpetual "punishment of eternal fire" is something the Christian deity deems just and fair (Jude 1:7). How is this loving in any way?

Blasphemers of the Holy Ghost are also on the guest list for damnation. The Bible says that "anyone who speaks...against the" Holy Spirit "will not be forgiven" of their sin (Matthew 12:32). Yahweh is willing to forgive "every kind of sin," including "blasphemy against" the Christian demigod (Matthew 12:31). Yet, if someone disrespects his ghost, he will "throw them into the blazing furnace, where there will be weeping and gnashing of teeth" (Matthew 13:50). They will never "be forgiven, either in this age or in the age to come" (Matthew 12:32). The loving Christian deity is either unable or unwilling to forgive those that say bad things about his ghost. Because of this he feels they deserve to "be tormented day and night for ever and ever" (Revelation 20:10).

The Bible says "whoever does not believe" in Yahweh and his son "stands condemned already" (John 3:18). If you do not believe, the Christian deity wants you to suffer forever. Yahweh's "wrath" will remain on "whoever rejects the Son" (John 3:36). Believe in me or perish. Know me or suffer. These are not the demands of a loving being.

Christians are caught up in an abusive relationship with an invisible man in the sky. Love and worship only me or suffer the perpetual "punishment of eternal fire," is not a gesture of kindness or mercy (Jude 1:7). Regardless of his threats with eternal torture, or how many children he has killed, they will never question their deity's actions. Christians are blind to the abuse, and they ignore the irrational threats of endless suffering. Why would anyone want to worship such a monster?

Chapter 10

Misrepresenting the Father of Lies

Within the Bible, there are stories and characters that Christians mistakenly affiliate with Satan. Some of these narratives have shaped his nature, origin, and appearance. Most Christians will tell you that Satan was one of Yahweh's most beautiful angels who became consumed by his pride and attempted to overthrow heaven. After the devil and his angels failed, Yahweh cast them out, sending "Satan" falling "like lightning from heaven" (Luke 10:18). Yet when we look into the verses that hold the source of these ideas, we find no mention of Satan at all. Every time the New Testament references the devil as a fallen angel, it is misusing narratives from the Old Testament that are clearly referencing human kings and not Satan.

The idea of Satan being an attractive outcast comes from two letters in the Old Testament, written to two separate kings. The first occurs in Ezekiel, where Yahweh writes a poem to the king of a place called Tyre: "Take up a lament concerning the king of Tyre and say to him: 'This is what Yahweh says'" (Ezekiel 28:12). This message is specifically addressed to the king of Tyre; no one else is ever mentioned.

In this lament, Yahweh accuses the king of calling himself "a god" (Ezekiel 28:2). The Christian deity wants him to know that despite his self-deification, he is just a man "and not a god" (Ezekiel 28:2). These verses are describing a human king who thinks very highly of himself. A man who has angered Yahweh with his pride, and not a fallen angel. This king is not Satan.

Yahweh continues his lament to the king of Tyre, calling him "a guardian cherub" who lived "on the holy mount of" Yahweh (Ezekiel 28:14). The king of Tyre is described as a model "of perfection, full of wisdom and perfect in beauty" (Ezekiel 28:12). The Bible says this king's "heart became proud on account of" his "beauty" and "splendor" (Ezekiel 28:17). His pride angered the Christian deity so much that he "threw" the king of Tyre "to the earth," making "a spectacle of" him "before kings" (Ezekiel 28:17). This is where Christians get the idea of Satan falling from heaven. Yet these verses do not reference anyone other than the king of Tyre. The devil is never mentioned, not once, but the king of Tyre is named several times. The main character in the storyline has to be replaced by Satan for the beautiful fallen angel concept to work. They have to add Satan to the story.

At one point in his sad poem, the Christian deity claims that the king of Tyre was "in Eden" (Ezekiel 28:13). After you replace the main character with Satan, this verse can now be used to substantiate the claim that Satan was in the garden of Eden. To fit the idea that Satan was the serpent who talked to Adam and Eve, the talking snake and Satan have to be added to the verse. According to Genesis, "the serpent was more crafty than any of the wild animals" Yahweh "had made" (Genesis 3:1). This verse is referring to an animal and not a king or Satan.

The curse Yahweh places on the serpent in the garden also contradicts the idea of it being Satan. Yahweh cursed the snake so that it would "crawl on" its "belly" and "eat dust all the days of" its "life" (Genesis 3:14). If the serpent in this narrative is, as many Christians believe it to be, the devil himself, they must admit that if the devil was cursed properly by Yahweh, he would be nothing more than a crafty legless dirt-eating creature. The devil, who Christians believe has feet, was either not the one who was cursed or found a way to break it. The Christian deity put a curse on a snake, cursing all snakes, not the devil, cursing all devils. This narrative does not, in any way, describe the Christian supervillain. This story does not reference Satan. Additionally, snakes don't eat dust, proving that either Yahweh's curse was ineffective or he never cursed all the snakes.

Just one chapter before his "lament" to the king of "Tyre," Yahweh writes "a lament" to the city of "Tyre" itself (Ezekiel 27:2). Yahweh describes the city of "Tyre" as being "perfect in beauty" (Ezekiel 27:3). Is this verse talking about the beauty and perfection of Satan or of a city? Do you think this verse is describing something or someone other than the city of Tyre? If you change the subject, the city of Tyre, and replace it with any magical being of your choosing, you are manipulating the verse by adding a character that was never there.

The book of Isaiah features another verse Christians mistakenly use to describe the devil's origin. Yahweh told one of his messengers to "take up" a "taunt against the king of Babylon" (Isaiah 14:4). Just like before, this verse is speaking about a specific individual and that one person is the king of Babylon and clearly not the devil. Yahweh told this human king that "the realm of the dead below is all astir to meet" him and that he had aroused "the spirits of the departed" (Isaiah 14:9). The Christian deity says that "maggots" will "spread out beneath" this king and that "worms" will "cover" him (Isaiah 14:11). This verse is clearly describing a mortal being of flesh and blood, not Satan.

Much like the king of Tyre, the Bible claims the king of Babylon wanted to "ascend to the heavens…raise" his "throne," and make himself "like the Most High," (Isaiah 14:13-14). This desire of the heart upset Yahweh, causing the king to be "cast down to the earth" (Isaiah 14:12). This is a threat written to an ancient king. Again, Satan is never mentioned. Nonetheless, most Christians will latch onto the language used in Isaiah that describes this king's descent into sin and attribute it to Satan's fall.

Yahweh calls the king of Babylon the "morning star, son of the dawn" (Isaiah 14:12). Most Christians believe the name Morning Star to be synonymous with the devil. Yet Jesus, their own demigod in sandals, called himself a morning star in Revelation. "I am the Root and the Offspring of David, and the bright Morning Star" (Revelation 22:16). Either their Jesus is calling himself Satan or the name Morning Star does not refer to Lucifer exclusively.

You cannot just change the main character of a story to fit your beliefs. These verses do not represent the devil. Nowhere at any point in Yahweh's taunt do we switch characters from the king of Babylon to anyone else. The person this threat was addressed to at the beginning is the exact same person it is addressing throughout.

Although the Bible does not give us an accurate description of Satan's origin, it does, however, describe his defeat. The pointless drama Yahweh has planned out for the Christian supervillain begins with an angel on his way to an "Abyss," carrying "a great chain" and a "key" from "heaven" (Revelation 20:1). Using this magical chain, the angel is going to seize "the devil…and bound him for a thousand years" (Revelation 20:1-2). "When a thousand years are over," Yahweh wants to release "Satan…from his prison" (Revelation 20:7). The loving, all-knowing Christian deity wants to release his archrival so that he "will go out" and "deceive the nations in the four corners of the earth" (Revelation 20:8). Ignoring the fact that the Bible claims the earth has four corners, Yahweh knew Satan would deceive large populations of people, causing their eternal damnation. He planned for this to happen; he took steps to accomplish this goal. How is this seen as a good thing?

The Bible says that after the devil is set free, he will "gather" an army so large "in number, they are like the sand on the seashore" (Revelation 20:8). Satan will combine forces with a prince named Gog and march his vast army "across the breadth of the earth" to "the camp of" Yahweh's "people, the city he loves" (Revelation 20:9). When the attackers reach the city and surround it, "fire" will come "down from heaven" to devour "them" (Revelation 20:9). Once the devil has done what the Christian deity created him to do, he will be tossed "into the lake of burning sulfur" (Revelation 20:10). Yahweh set these events into motion; he is the only reason these armies showed up to destroy the Israelites. Yahweh creates "disaster," unleashes it, and then wants to be praised for stopping it (Isaiah 45:7).

The release of Satan served no purpose apart from Yahweh wanting to show off his powers. He chose to do this. What if I made a creature whose entire purpose was to cause death and destruction everywhere it went? What if I set this destructive creature free just to show people how powerful I am when I stop it? Would I be worthy of praise and glory? Would you find me competent and loving?

The one who creates evil with the intention of unleashing it upon the world is not the good guy in the story. That person, that being, by the basic laws of most countries would be held accountable for knowingly creating and freeing something dangerous. Once Yahweh creates and releases evil, he is the one responsible for all that it does. He created the problem, and instead of keeping it locked up, he thought it would be a great idea to let it out.

The Bible says that Satan is "the father of lies" and that "when he lies, he speaks his native language" (John 8:44). Yet when one reads the Bible, they find this accusation to be false. Nowhere in the Bible does Satan actually lie. Yahweh, however, lies throughout. He lies from the very beginning about his magical tree and the effects of its fruit in Genesis 2. He sends "a deceiving spirit" to "prophets" in an attempt to send a man named Ahab to his demise (1 Kings 22:22). In 2 Thessalonians he purposely deceives the Jewish people by sending "them a powerful delusion so that they will believe the lie," condemning them all (2 Thessalonians 2:11). How can a being be both a liar and perfect?

As an all-knowing being, Yahweh should be able to recognize when the devil is trying to influence or persuade him. Satan should not be able to convince the Christian deity to do anything harmful or villainous. Yet, when we look at the story of Job, we find Yahweh falling into temptation. We find that Satan is able to trick his creator into allowing him to kill and destroy.

Job was one of Yahweh's biggest fans. He "was blameless and upright; he feared God and shunned evil" (Job 1:1). He was a loyal follower through and through. On account of his undying devotion, the Christian deity "blessed" Job "so that his flocks and herds" were "spread throughout the land" (Job 1:10). He liked Job, and Satan knew it.

"One day," Satan and a bunch of "angels" presented "themselves before" Yahweh (Job 1:6). Completely ignoring every angel in the room that came to see him, Yahweh turned to the devil and asked him "where" he had "come from" (Job 1:7). Yahweh failed to be all-knowing when he did not know where his arch-nemesis had been and needed to ask him. Satan responded to Yahweh, stating that he had been "going back and forth on" the earth (Job 1:7). Yahweh accepted this answer and quickly changed the subject. He asked Satan if he had ever noticed that super great guy, Job, before. Yahweh began to brag about his super fan, telling Satan that "there is no one on earth like him" (Job 1:8).

"Does Job fear" Yahweh "for nothing?" Satan inquired (Job 1:9). Pressing him further, Satan asked the all-knowing Christian deity, if Yahweh were to "stretch out" his "hand and strike everything" Job "has," instead of allowing him to prosper, would Job not "curse" him instead of praising him (Job 1:11). Yahweh, completely ignorant of what the result of this pointless test would be, told the Christian bad guy, "Very well, then, everything he has is in your power" (Job 1:12). Yahweh failed to know the answer to Satan's question and allowed his nemesis access to his creations for the sole purpose of testing this man's loyalty to him. Instead of entertaining the idea of a loyalty test, the Christian deity should have told the devil to go kick rocks. If Yahweh knew Job's heart, then he would not have been incited by the devil to establish a fact he should have already known.

While Job was resting at home one evening, minding his own business, a messenger came bearing some bad news for him. The messenger told Job that a group of people called "the Sabeans attacked and" carried "off" all of his oxen and donkeys and then "put" his "servants to the sword" (Job 1:15). "While" that messenger "was still speaking, another messenger came and said," that "the fire of God fell from the heavens and burned up" his "sheep and" his "servants" (Job 1:16). Did the Christian deity give Satan access to his personal fire, or was Yahweh himself responsible for the pyrotechnics? Whether it was Satan or Yahweh that discharged the holy flame, the point is that somebody used it and that these people died horribly because of the ignorance of the Christian deity, because of his inability to know the answer to Satan's question.

"While" the second messenger "was still speaking another messenger came and," told Job that "the Chaldeans" (or Babylonians) grabbed all of his "camels and" carried them "off," and then put his "servants to the sword" (Job 1:17). "While" that messenger "was still speaking, yet another messenger came and said," that "a mighty wind swept in from the desert and" destroyed "the house" where his seven "sons" and three "daughters" were having dinner, killing everyone inside (Job 1:18-19). Yahweh gave Satan permission to kill a man's servants and family for the sole purpose of testing his loyalty.

Despite everything the Christian deity put "Job" through, he "did not sin by" saying Yahweh did anything wrong (Job 1:22). Yahweh admits that he thinks "Job" kept "his integrity" by not blaming him for being tricked by "Satan" (Job 2:3). Yahweh believes Job demonstrated moral soundness by not calling him out on his fatal mistake. This is the mindset of the being that Christians worship. The story of Job points out that it is sinful to accuse Yahweh of any wrongdoing. He does not want you to blame him when he tests your loyalty by sending a bad guy to kill your kids. It is not Yahweh's fault Job's servants were set on fire, because Satan made him do it.

Once again, "the angels came to present themselves before the Lord, and Satan came with them" (Job 2:1). Yahweh, once more, ignorantly asks the devil, "where" he had "come from" (Job 2:2). Giving the same answer as the last time Yahweh had asked, Satan replies that he was "going back and forth on" the earth (Job 2:2). Yahweh changes the subject and begins to brag about his favorite human "Job," repeating his previous compliments (Job 2:3). This time at the end of all his gloating, Yahweh becomes aware that he has fallen for one of the devil's schemes. He tells Satan that Job "still maintains his integrity, though" Satan has "incited" him "against" Job "to ruin him without any reason" (Job 2:3). Although Yahweh claims to be aware of the trickery, Satan is still able to talk the all-knowing Christian deity into pointlessly causing Job harm.

Satan told Yahweh the reason Job chose not to "curse" his name was because he did not "strike his flesh and bones" (Job 2:5). Satan now wanted Yahweh to cause Job physical harm to find out if he would "curse" him or not (Job 2:5). Yahweh thought this was a fantastic idea, saying, "Very well, then, he is in your hands" (Job 2:6). The all-knowing Christian deity took the devil's suggestion to test his creation's allegiance by torturing him.

With Yahweh's approval, "Satan went out…and afflicted Job with painful sores from the soles of his feet to the crown of his head" (Job 2:7). Yahweh was concerned that his number one fan might sin by yelling at him for causing the painful sores and the deaths of his children and servants. "In all this, Job did not sin with what he said" (Job 2:10). He did not curse Yahweh for causing him so much pain and suffering.

"Satan" was somehow able to provoke the all-knowing Christian deity to the point of destroying a man's life "without any reason" (Job 2:3). Through his own ignorance, Yahweh permitted the devil to kill countless innocent people. If Yahweh is an all-powerful and all-knowing being as his book states he is, then he had the power and the knowledge to prevent the deaths he caused through his own incompetence. If he did not know, he ceases to be all-knowing. If Yahweh knows everything, then he would already know the extent of Job's loyalty without having to test it. If Yahweh is all-knowing, then he knew the consequences of his actions; he knew that releasing Satan to experiment on Job would be the direct cause of countless fatalities. Yahweh "does whatever pleases him" (Psalm 135:6) and allowing the devil to set fire to Job's servants and crush his children was pleasing to the Christian deity, or he would not have permitted their senseless deaths.

Yahweh did not have to create evil or Satan. The deity that claims to have limitless power and infinite knowledge could have chosen from an endless number of options. Yet he decided to design and build his own enemy. The Christian deity wanted the pointless drama of having an evil entity running around infecting people, causing them to fall into sin, and damning them to an eternal stay at his personal palace of pain. The deity Christians want you to worship continuously chooses death and destruction instead of love and compassion. These are not the actions of a loving, caring being. We "are regarded as nothing" and "he does as he pleases with the powers of heaven and the peoples of the earth" (Daniel 4:35). Why would anyone want to worship such a monster?

Chapter 11

Penis Jacket

The Christian deity demands complete devotion from his creations. He requires them to obey his every command, no matter how absurd or horrific. He decided he would need some kind of promise from them, some sort of barbaric loyalty test. Being an all-knowing deity, every possible method or procedure that these people could do or say to pledge their fealty to him had been taken into account. Yahweh settled on the idea he thought was best. He was going to need every man to cut off part of their penis. Nothing shows your commitment to a cause quite like mutilating your own genitals.

Yahweh tried out his new loyalty test on one of his favorite people, Abraham. Abraham was a huge Yahweh fan and willing to do anything the Christian deity asked of him. Yahweh told Abraham that he was going to make a covenant with him, but in return, he needed him to chop off part of his penis. Yahweh wanted him "to undergo circumcision" as a "sign of the covenant between" them (Genesis 17:11). Abraham followed this painfully pointless new rule and circumcised himself and "his son Isaac" when he "was eight days old" (Genesis 21:4). Yahweh explains to Abraham that "the covenant" he is "to keep" is that "every male" in his town, must "be circumcised" as well (Genesis 17:10). Why would anyone follow a being that claims to know everything yet requires you to slice up your genitals to prove your loyalty?

Yahweh does not like that extra skin on the penis; he finds it offensive. He told Abraham that all "uncircumcised" men will not be allowed to hang out with any of the "circumcised" men (Genesis 17:14). They "will be cut off from" their "people" (Genesis 17:14). Even the foreigners "residing among" Yahweh's people who want "to celebrate" his "Passover must have all the males in" their "household circumcised" (Exodus 12:48). Show your allegiance by cutting your genitals, and Yahweh will allow you to attend his party, commemorating the time he killed "all the firstborn" kids "in Egypt" while they were sleeping in their beds (Exodus 12:29).

According to Exodus 4, the foreskin can be used to deter the murderous impulses of the Christian deity. Still holding onto a grudge against Moses for not taking the job he had offered him, Yahweh decided that it was time for him to die. The Christian deity waited until Moses arrived at "a lodging place" to make his move (Exodus 4:24). With anger in his heart and murder on his mind, Yahweh "met Moses" at "a lodging place" intending "to kill him" (Exodus 4:24). Fortunately for Moses, his wife was there holding their infant son. Realizing what was about to happen, Moses' wife "took a flint knife, cut off her son's foreskin and touched Moses' feet with it" (Exodus 4:25). Once she had slapped her husband's feet with a bloody chunk of her son's penis, she said some special words, and Yahweh "let him alone" (Exodus 4:26). The Christian deity halted his murderous action because someone cut off a piece of a child's penis and rubbed it onto the feet of the victim to be. There may be some kind of strange connection between Yahweh and the repelling power of foreskin. Perhaps foreskin is to Yahweh as green rocks are to a certain superhero?

In 1 Samuel 18, before he was king of Israel, the biblical hero, David, purchased the daughter of the current king, King Saul, using the foreskins of his enemies. The "price" Saul had set for his daughter's hand in marriage was one "hundred Philistine foreskins" (1 Samuel 18:25). David, being a persistent overachiever, returned with "two hundred" Philistine "foreskins," and presented them to his king

(1 Samuel 18:27). After which, "Saul gave him his daughter Michal in marriage" (1 Samuel 18:27).

The Old Testament focuses mainly on disfiguring one's penis to show your loyalty. In the New Testament, however, Yahweh or Paul seems to struggle with the idea of circumcision. The Bible says that Abraham was blessed and that Yahweh "will never count" his sins "against" him (Romans 4:8). He claims that Abraham was credited with righteousness, "not after, but before" "he was circumcised" (Romans 4:10). According to the New Testament, Yahweh changed his mind and decided that he no longer needs people to chop off parts of their genitals to prove their dedication to him. According to Yahweh's own breathed out words, "circumcision is nothing," and the only thing that matters is "keeping" his "commands" (1 Corinthians 7:19).

Yahweh, at one point in his bizarre novel, declares that "every man who lets himself be circumcised...is obligated to obey the whole law" (Galatians 5:3). Whether your circumcision was the result of your parents' decision or your own, the Christian deity states that "circumcision" only "has value if you observe the law" (Romans 2:25). "But if you break the law, you have become as though you had not been circumcised" at all (Romans 2:25). Defy one of Yahweh's perfect laws, and your carved up penis now serves no purpose. This new rule might have been a useful amendment to the rules Yahweh set up way back in the Old Testament, when he told his favorite people all that they needed to do was cut themselves in order to prove their loyalty to him. Maybe Yahweh should add a disclaimer that reads: "If you decide to mutilate yourselves for the cause, you must also be willing to follow every ridiculous rule Yahweh deemed perfect or your pain and suffering will have been in vain." Why wait until centuries later to add to the order?

The Bible says that through the death of the Christian deity's son, we "were also circumcised" in the releasing of the sinful nature, not "with a circumcision" done "by" the "hands" of men but "with" the "circumcision" done by Jesus (Colossians 2:11). Yahweh is now a firm believer that his son's death was a form of circumcision, cutting off one's sins as if it were some kind of foreskin. The Christian demigod, through his bloodshed, saved us from the wrath of Yahweh and genital mutilation.

The Christian deity is obsessed with the act of circumcision. He even uses it throughout his book to form odd metaphors. Yahweh tells us in Jeremiah 4, "circumcise your hearts...or" his "wrath will flare up and burn like fire because of the evil you have done" (Jeremiah 4:4). The bible says that if you do not remove the foreskin of "your heart" on your own, then Yahweh will be forced to "circumcise your hearts and the hearts of your descendants, so that you may love him" (Deuteronomy 30:6). Foreskin disturbs him so much he wants it removed from everywhere, your penis, your heart, and even your "ears" (Acts 7:51).

In the span of the Old Testament to the New Testament, the Christian deity takes his bizarre idea of genital disfigurement from loyalty test to analogy. Ultimately, he fails to be all-knowing when he needs you to prove your commitment to the cause and he fails to be loving when he requires his people to cut off their penis jacket. Why would anyone want to advocate for a being that wants you to pointlessly slice off parts of your genitals? Why would anyone want worship such a monster!?

Chapter 12

The Scent of an Apology

Before he sent himself to die, the Christian deity required his people to apologize to him by killing animals and performing blood magic. By using the death of an innocent in exchange for a pardon. This barbaric system's first appearance in the Bible can be found within the legend of Cain and Abel. Cain and Abel were the first human brothers to be born on Yahweh's new planet. "Abel kept flocks, and Cain worked the soil" (Genesis 4:2). One day the two brothers went before their deity, and because "no one is to appear before" Yahweh "empty-handed," they presented him with gifts (Exodus 34:20). "Cain brought some of the fruits of the soil," and Abel, who was the keeper of animals, killed "some of the firstborn of his flock" and "brought" Yahweh the "fat portions" for his "offering" (Genesis 4:3-4). The Christian deity "looked with favor on Abel and his offering, but on Cain and his offering, he did not look with favor" (Genesis 4:4-5). Knowing the consequences of his actions, Yahweh made the decision to reject both the gift and the man.

The rejection that came from his deity made "Cain...very angry" (Genesis 4:5). Yahweh told his offended creation that "if" he did "what" was "right," he would "be accepted" (Genesis 4:6). Giving the Christian deity the fat of a slaughtered animal was the right thing to do. Giving him broccoli was the wrong thing to do. Yahweh would not tolerate an offering of vegetation from Cain; he needs blood and body parts, or he will not accept you.

After his inspirational conversation with Yahweh, "Cain attacked his brother Abel and killed him" (Genesis 4:8). Yahweh knew this would happen. He knew his act of rejection would bring about the first murder, and still, he chose to look at Cain's offering unfavorably. He chose death.

Needing a place to receive his gifts of blood and death, Yahweh invented the altar. The first "altar" Yahweh sent down plans for was to be made "of earth" (Exodus 20:24). If there was not enough dirt nearby to complete the mound, and they were forced to use rocks, he forbade them from using "dressed stones" (Exodus 20:25). "Dressed stones" required the use of "a tool," and tools, according to Yahweh, "will defile" his "altar" (Exodus 20:25). Lastly, Yahweh did not want his people to put any stairs on his altar. He did not want their "private parts" to be "exposed" on it (Exodus 20:26).

One day Yahweh decided he wanted to "dwell among" his people, so he asked his creations to build him an earthly house (Exodus 25:8). For this, Yahweh required a new, unique altar. Something flashier than a simple dirt mound. This time around, he wanted his "altar" to be covered in "bronze" (Exodus 27:2-3).

Yahweh wanted his "altar" to be made of "acacia wood," with horns placed "at each of the four corners" (Exodus 27:1-2). He wanted every pot used "to remove the ashes, and its shovels," and all the "sprinkling bowls, meat forks and firepans," to be bronzed (Exodus 27:3). Yahweh wanted "a bronze network" of "grating" and "a bronze ring at each of the four corners" (Exodus 27:4). He even wanted "the poles of acacia wood" to be "bronze" (Exodus 27:6). Why did Yahweh choose bronze? Does that specific element serve a magical purpose, or did it make it easier to wash all the blood off? Perhaps Yahweh, or the person who came up with this idea, really liked the color bronze.

The gory apologetic system Yahweh chose to implement consisted of a variety of blood rituals. For his burnt offerings, Yahweh required "an animal from either the herd or the flock" (Leviticus

1:2). If the sacrificial animal came "from the herd" it had to be "a male without defect" (Leviticus 1:3) Yahweh needed his people to "present" the animal to him "at the entrance to" his personal tent, "the tent of meeting" (Leviticus 1:3). Standing in front of Yahweh's tent, the sacrificer, the person sending the apology to Yahweh, must place their "hand on the head of the burnt offering" (Leviticus 1:4). Only then will the dead animal "be accepted on" their "behalf to make atonement" (Leviticus 1:4).

Once the animal was approved as an acceptable apology, the Christian deity had them "slaughter the young bull" in front of him (Leviticus 1:5). He told them to collect "the blood" from the "bull" and "splash it against the sides of the altar" (Leviticus 1:5). The splashing of blood onto the bronze was required if you wanted to be forgiven. He needed the blood splashed.

After they sprinkled the altar, Yahweh wanted them "to skin the" animal "and cut it into pieces" (Leviticus 1:6). They were to take their dismembered apology, "including the head and the fat," and place it "on the wood that" was burning on the altar" (Leviticus 1:8). While that was cooking, he wanted them "to wash the internal organs and the legs with water," and then "burn all of" that "on the altar" as well (Leviticus 1:9) The burning meat created "an aroma" that was "pleasing to the" Christian deity (Leviticus 1:9). He loved the smell of a good apology.

If "anyone" sinned "unintentionally and" did something that was "forbidden," Yahweh required a different kind of offering from them, one he called the "sin offering" (Leviticus 4:2-3). If the accidental sinner was one of his "anointed priests," then he was to "bring...a young bull without defect" to "the tent of" Yahweh (Leviticus 4:3-4). Once there, the priest was "to lay his hand on its head and slaughter it before" his loving deity (Leviticus 4:4). Yahweh required the priest to then "dip his fingers into the blood and sprinkle some of it seven times...in front of" his special "curtain" (Leviticus 4:6). He wanted them to "put some of the blood on the horns of" a separate altar, "the altar of fragrant incense," and then "pour out" the rest of the blood "at the base of the altar of burning" (Leviticus

4:7). He wanted "all the fat from the bull" removed and burned "on the altar of burnt offering" (Leviticus 4:8-10). "The rest of the bull" had to be taken "outside the camp" and burned "in a wood fire on the ash heap" (Leviticus 4:12).

"If the whole Israelite community" sinned, Yahweh wanted them to "bring a young bull" to his "tent…lay their hands on the bulls head" and slaughter it in front of him (Leviticus 4:14-15). "The anointed priest" was "to take some of the bull's blood…dip his finger into the blood and sprinkle it before" Yahweh's special "curtain" "seven times" (Leviticus 4:16-17). He wanted them "to put some of the blood on the horns of the altar" in front of him, and "the rest of the blood" he wanted to be poured "out at the base of the altar of burnt offerings" (Leviticus 4:18). Once the blood had been sprinkled in the places that Yahweh liked it to be sprinkled, the priest was to "remove all the fat from it and burn it on the altar" (Leviticus 4:19). This was how the priest was to make "atonement for them" (Leviticus 4:19). This is how the loving Christian deity wanted his people to say they were sorry to him.

If "a leader" sinned "unintentionally and" did something "forbidden," he had to "bring" to Yahweh's tent "a male goat without defect…lay his hands on the goat's head and slaughter it at the place where the burnt" offerings were "slaughtered" (Leviticus 4:22-24). "The priest" was to "take some of the blood," dip his finger in it, "and put it on the horns of the altar" (Leviticus 4:25). Yahweh then wanted the priest to "pour out the rest of the blood at the base of the altar" (Leviticus 4:25). With the blood properly applied to the locations Yahweh needs them applied to, he wanted "all the fat" to be burned "on the altar" (Leviticus 4: 26). "In this way, the priest will make atonement for the leader's sin, and he will be forgiven" (Leviticus 4:26).

"If any" single "member of the community" sinned "unintentionally and" did something "forbidden," he was to "bring…a female goat without defect" to Yahweh's tent, "lay their hand on the head of the" goat and then "slaughter it" (Leviticus 4:28-29). Once the animal had been slaughtered in front of the Christian deity, he required "the priest…to take some of the blood with his finger and put it on the horns of the altar of burnt offering" (Leviticus 4:30). After the blood had been applied to the horns, they were to "pour out the rest of the blood at the base of the altar" (Leviticus 4:30). "All the fat" was to be "removed" and burned "on the altar as an aroma" that was "pleasing to the" Christian deity (Leviticus 4:31). All of this must be performed, just so they can "be forgiven" by their perfect, bloodthirsty deity (Leviticus 4:31).

Yahweh also needed a fellowship or peace offering presented to him. Exceedingly similar to the sin offering and the burnt offering, this particular blood ritual required the followers of Yahweh to "present before" him "an animal without defect" (Leviticus 3:1). The person who was offering the animal up as a magical living apology was again told "to lay" their "hand on the head of" the animal "and slaughter it at the entrance to" their deity's personal "tent" (Leviticus 3:2). Yahweh needs to see a living being die, he has to witness the blood get sprinkled "against the sides of the altar" (Leviticus 3:2). He needed "all the fat" removed and burned "on the altar" (Leviticus 3:3-5). Whether the peace "offering" brought to him is "a lamb" or "a goat," Yahweh finds the smell of these burning animals to be "a pleasing aroma" (Leviticus 3:5-16).

The Christian deity wanted a monthly offering, a little something extra on the first of the month. For these monthly offerings, he required "two young bulls, one ram and seven male lambs a year old, all without defect" (Numbers 28:11). For his special "Sabbath day," Yahweh felt he deserved an additional "offering of two lambs" (Numbers 28:9). He wanted "guilt" offerings (Leviticus 5:14-19) and "wave" offerings (Leviticus 7:30). Why would a loving being call for the slaughter of so many life forms for so many pointless rituals? Why is he so picky about how and when his creations say they are sorry? Spill the blood, sprinkle the blood, now burn the flesh, and then the Christian deity will be able to forgive you, exonerating all of your sinful acts through the power of blood magic. Why can he not simply forgive without all of the theatrics?

Thirty-seven times, the Bible mentions Yahweh's fondness for the smell of his charred apologies: Genesis 8:21, Exodus 29:18, Exodus 29:25, Exodus 29:41, Leviticus 1:9, Leviticus 1:13, Leviticus 1:17, Leviticus 2:2, Leviticus 2:9, Leviticus 2:12, Leviticus 3:5, Leviticus 3:16, Leviticus 4:31, Leviticus 6:15, Leviticus 6:21, Leviticus 8:21, Leviticus 17:6, Leviticus 23:13, Leviticus 23:18, Numbers 15:3, Numbers 15:7, Numbers 15:10, Numbers 15:13, Numbers 15:14, Numbers 15:24, Numbers 18:17, Numbers 28:2, Numbers 28:6, Numbers 28:8, Numbers 28:13, Numbers 28:24, Numbers 28:27, Numbers 29:2, Numbers 29:6, Numbers 29:8, Numbers 29:13, and Numbers 29:36. Why is Yahweh so obsessed with the smell of burning flesh? Is there no barbecue in heaven? Or is it the smell of the blood specifically and not necessarily the flesh itself? According to Leviticus, "blood" has been "given" to us by Yahweh "to make atonement…on the altar" (Leviticus 17:11). Blood is intended to be used in this way. Any other interaction or ingestion of the "blood" is strictly forbidden (Leviticus 17:12). Or does Yahweh just enjoy the killing being done in his name? This form of sacrifice, the slaughtering of an innocent, is not only pleasing to Yahweh, but a required action if one is to stay on the good side of this self-absorbed deity.

The Christian deity loved his grotesque apologetic system so much that he incorporated it into a variety of ceremonies and symbolic promises. For instance, if one wishes to become a priest, Yahweh requires the slaughter of an assortment of animals. To begin the priestly purification process, or the PPP for short, Yahweh will need his people to bring him "a young bull and two rams," bread and cakes "with olive oil mixed in," and wafers spread "with olive oil" (Exodus 29:1-2). He needs them to wear special garments, including "a turban" with a "plate" made "of pure gold" inscribed with the words "Holy to the Lord" (Exodus 39:30-31).

Once they had their Yahweh-approved outfits on, he wanted them to "bring the bull to the…entrance" of his "tent" and "slaughter it" (Exodus 29:10-11). He required them to "take some of the bull's blood and put it on the horns of the altar with" their fingers "and pour out the rest of it at the base of the altar" (Exodus 29:12). He wanted "the fat on the internal organs, the" covering "of the liver, and both kidneys" to be burned "on the altar" (Exodus 29:13). The "bull's flesh and its hide" were to be burned as "a sin offering" (Exodus 29:14).

Next, they were to "take one of the rams...lay their hands on its head," and "slaughter it" (Exodus 29:15-16). The Christian deity wanted the blood of the ram to be sprinkled "against the sides of the altar" (Exodus 29:16). After the blood had been splashed, they were to "cut the ram into pieces and...burn" it all "on the altar," appeasing the Christian deity with its "pleasing aroma" (Exodus 29:18). This was to be the "burnt offering" (Exodus 29:18). They were to bring the last blood offering, "the other ram...lay their hands on its head" and "slaughter it" so that Yahweh could see it happen (Exodus 29:19-20). He wanted them to "take some of its blood and put it on the lobes of" their "right ears...on the thumbs of their right hands, and on the big toes of their right feet" (Exodus 29:20). They were to take the rest of "its blood" and "splash" it "against the sides of the altar" (Exodus 29:20). Once the blood was applied to the proper body parts, Yahweh told them to mix "some of the blood with some of the anointing oil and sprinkle it on" the pre-priests and their "garments," magically turning them into "consecrated" priests with holy clothing (Exodus 29:21).

This was the process Yahweh chose to implement. The loving Christian deity wanted people to slaughter animals and put blood on themselves. Why was he so specific about where and how to perform his rituals? Would the magic not work if the blood was placed on the wrong ear or toe? What if the blood dripped or spilled in the wrong area? How would Yahweh handle this inevitable situation?

Obsessed with his bloody apologetic system, Yahweh required his followers to "make atonement for the altar" itself (Exodus 29:37). He demanded an apology for his grill. "As a sin offering," the Christian deity wanted his people to "sacrifice a bull" on behalf of "the altar" every "day...for seven days," after which "the altar will be most holy, and whatever touches it will be holy" as well (Exodus 29:36-

105

37). These are the commands of a crazy person, not a perfect, loving being. How does an inanimate object sin? What could it possibly have done to be sorry for?

Additionally, the Christian deity taught his followers how to use this apologetic blood ritual to summon a burst of Yahweh fire from heaven. For this to happen, the Christian deity needed his followers to kill more animals, spilling and sprinkling their blood in all the places that he requires it to be sprinkled and spilled for the spell to work. Blood must be shed before Yahweh will appear as a flame; he will not show up if multiple life forms are not slaughtered.

The loving Christian deity wanted "a bull calf…a ram…a male goat…a calf and a lamb—both a year old and without defect…an ox and" another "ram" to be slaughtered "before" him (Leviticus 9:2-4). The "calf" was to be "slaughtered" first (Leviticus 9:8). Yahweh wanted his people to dip their fingers into its "blood and" place "it on the horns of the altar," pouring "the rest of the blood" onto "the base" (Leviticus 9:9). Next, they were to slaughter the ram, calf, and lamb, sprinkling their blood "against the sides of the altar" (Leviticus 9:12). The goat," then "the ox and the" other "ram" were to be slaughtered, and their blood splashed "against the sides of the altar" (Leviticus 9:15-18). Yahweh needed them to take "the fat portions of the ox and the ram—the fat tail, the layer of fat, the kidneys and the" covering "of the liver," and lay them all "on the breasts" of the animals (Leviticus 9:19-20). They were to take the "breasts and the right thigh," it had to be the right thigh or it would not work, and "wave" them "before the" Christian deity "as a wave offering" (Leviticus 9:21). Yahweh literally wanted them to wave pieces of a dead animal at him. What did the waving of body parts directly at him accomplish? What purpose did it serve in the mind of Yahweh? Is he unable to proceed, is he not capable of completing the spell, until he sees them waving a butchered animal?

Once all of the animals had been killed and all of the blood splattered on all the right places, Yahweh would shoot out "fire" and consume "the burnt offering and the fat portions" that were cooking "on the altar" (Leviticus 9:24). What kind of being needs animals killed

106

in order to show up for your barbecue? Is Yahweh not able to accept a verbal or written invitation? Why did he require the use of blood magic?

The animals for these rituals had to be flawless "in order" for them to "be accepted" (Leviticus 22:19). "The blind, the injured or maimed, or anything with warts or festering or running sores" or "whose testicles" had been "bruised, crushed, torn or cut" were all unacceptable to the Christian deity (Leviticus 22:22-25). He did not want "an ox or a sheep that" had "any defect or flaw in it, for" he found these things to "be detestable" (Deuteronomy 17:1). Due to his exaggerated sense of self-importance, Yahweh thought he deserved to have perfect animals slaughtered to him.

At one point, Yahweh got annoyed with the quality of animals being brought to him. He asked his followers, "If I am a father, where is the honor due me? If I am a master, where is the respect due me?" (Malachi 1:6). The Christian deity felt he had been disrespected; he thought his people had shown "contempt for" his "name" by serving him defective apologies (Malachi 1:6). Crippled "or diseased animals" were being sacrificed and passed off as acceptable blood payments (Malachi 1:8). They were putting "defiled food on" his special grill (Malachi 1:7).

Yahweh asked his people, "When you offer blind animals for sacrifice, is that not wrong? When you sacrifice lame or diseased animals, is that not wrong? Try offering them to your governor! Would he be pleased with you? Would he accept you?" (Malachi 1:8). They had to kill and burn the best animals they had to Yahweh, or he would not accept them.

After all of his warnings, Yahweh still received blemished offerings. Frustrated with his people, he told them, "If you do not listen, and if you do not resolve to honor my name, I will send a curse upon you, and I will curse your blessings...because of you I will rebuke your descendants; I will smear on your faces the dung from your festival sacrifices" (Malachi 2:1-3). Why would the Christian deity want to smear poop on someone's face? Do these sound like the actions of a perfect being or a self-absorbed toddler?

Eventually, Yahweh grew tired of getting diseased goats. So he made it "impossible for the blood of bulls and goats to take away sins" (Hebrews 10:4). He altered his apologetic system. No longer would mere animals suffice as an apology. Yahweh knew this was going to happen. He planned for it to happen this way. Why would he not start off with the perfect system?

The Christian deity was "not pleased" with the "burnt offerings and sin offerings" he was receiving, he yearned for something more (Hebrews 10:6). Yahweh desired the slaughter of perfect beings, and to him, there was nothing more perfect than himself. With much deliberation and thought, the Christian deity determined that he would have to send himself in human form to die. This was the best idea that he could come up with, this was his perfect plan. "For" Yahweh "so loved the world that he" wanted to save it from what he was going to do to it if flawless blood was not shed (John 3:16). So he sent his "only Son," or himself in the form of Jesus, to die (John 3:16). The Bible then says that "whoever believes" this happened will be saved from being thrown into the fiery torture chamber created by the loving Christian deity (John 3:16). If the plan was to have Jesus be the perfect sacrifice, why not start off with that? Why did Yahweh require the wrong blood for so long?

The Bible says that Jesus "died as a ransom" (Hebrews 9:15). A ransom to who? Who did Jesus save us from? Yahweh. Why? Because the Christian deity cannot stop himself, he cannot control his anger without the shedding of innocent blood. Someone's blood had to be spilled in order for the world to "be saved" from Yahweh's "wrath" (Romans 5:9). Christians seem to have no issue with this. They see the actions and desires of their deity as a good thing. They want the world to bow down and be subservient to him. They want your children to be washed in the blood of their demigod.

The loving Christian deity is the one who made the rule that "without the shedding of blood there is no forgiveness" (Hebrews 9:22). He did not have to make that rule. If Yahweh was all-powerful and loving, he would be able to accept an apology without a dramatic show of repentance by pointlessly slaughtering life forms. Why can he not accept flowers, letters, or even a simple verbal apology? Why is that so hard for a loving, caring being to do?

In order to appease his hurt feelings and thirst for perfect blood, the Christian deity impregnated a human being using his ghost, creating a demigod that would later be slaughtered as a sacrifice to him. Yahweh's master plan was to magically transform the blood of a demigod into an apology he would be willing to accept for all mankind. Yahweh is so angry at you for using the supposed free will he gave you, that the only way to subdue his wrath and prevent the eternal punishment he has waiting for you is to spill the blood of the innocent in his presence. He wanted to watch his own son die for his inability to accept a simple apology. These are not the actions of someone who is worthy of respect and admiration. How can anyone find these demands to be virtuous or honorable? Why would anyone want to worship such a monster?

Chapter 13

The Musical Apocalypse

The end is inevitable, no one can escape its slow and steady approach. It has been prophesied and predicted by multitudes of charismatic charlatans, all claiming knowledge of some unknown future event or action that will extinguish all life as we know it. Christianity carries its own set of apocalyptic ideas and beliefs. Blueprints for the end of the world.

In the book of Daniel, Yahweh tells us through his prophet, through his mouthpiece, that the end of the world "will be a time of distress such as has not happened" before (Daniel 12:1). The dead "will awake" to either their "everlasting life" or their "everlasting contempt" (Daniel 12:2). Unlike most of the Bible messengers carrying news of the end, Daniel did not believe that these things would come to pass in his lifetime. He spoke of these events as if they were to take place in the distant future.

Paul, another one of those important figures within the Christian religion, wrote some letters to various churches, using Yahweh-given predictions, explaining what the end of the world would be like under the current deistic management. He wrote to the church in Ephesus, warning of the "terrible times" that will be had by all during "the last days" (2 Timothy 3:1). Paul also wrote a letter to a church in Corinth telling them that they "will not all sleep," and that "in a flash, in the twinkling of an eye, at the last trumpet...the dead will be raised" and they "will be changed" (1 Corinthians 15:51-52).

In another letter, this time to the "church of the Thessalonians," (1 Thessalonians 1:1), Paul claimed that Jesus "himself will come down from heaven" (1 Thessalonians 4:16). And with a magic "trumpet call," all of "the dead" who followed Yahweh when they were alive, all of the Christians, "will rise" up out of their graves and float up to the clouds (1 Thessalonians 4:16). Paul thought he and the recipients of his letters were going to "be caught up together in the clouds" with the deceased believers (1 Thessalonians 4:17).

Unlike Daniel, Paul firmly believed that he and his friends were going to witness the second coming of Jesus within his lifetime. He thought he was going to observe and take part in the events leading up to and during the last days. He was not going to sleep; he was going to hear the last trumpet call. Paul was wrong, of course, just like those before him and the countless that will follow.

The Christian demigod himself prophesied the end times. When leaving the temple one day, the twelve disciples pointed out all of the "magnificent buildings" that were around them (Mark 13:1). Deciding to give his followers some insight into the end of the world, "Jesus" told them that eventually "not one stone" would "be left on another; every one" of them will eventually "be thrown down" (Mark 13:2). Curious about the destruction of the temple buildings, his disciples asked him, "when...these things" would "happen, and what" "the sign that they are all about to be fulfilled" would be (Mark 13:4). Jesus warned them that there would be deceivers in those days, saying that "many" would "come in" his "name" (Luke 21:8). His disciples themselves would "hear of wars and rumors of wars," and "nation" would "rise against nation and kingdom against kingdom" (Mark 13:7-8). He told them that there" would "be great earthquakes, famines and pestilences in various places, and fearful events and great signs from heaven" (Luke 21:11). Jesus called these events "the beginning of birth pains" (Mark 13:8).

Jesus informed his disciples that during these times, "brother will betray brother" and "children will rebel against their parents and have them put to death" (Mark 13:12). He warned them that "the sun will be darkened, and the moon will not give its light; the stars will fall from the sky" (Mark 13:24-25). After Yahweh removes all light sources, he tells us that the entire planet will somehow be able to "see the Son of Man," or Jesus, "coming in clouds" (Mark 13:26). When the Christian demigod returns, he is going to be riding on a cloud in complete darkness.

Jesus believed that his disciples would be rounded up, "flogged in the synagogues" (Mark 13:9), and "hated by all nations" (Matthew 24:9). "Everyone will hate" the twelve "because of" Jesus (Mark 13:13). He thought his disciples were going to take part in Yahweh's apocalypse, just as Paul thought he and his church members were going to float up into the clouds with their deceased Christian brothers and sisters. Clearly, this did not happen. Jesus was wrong.

The Christian demigod proceeded to tell his followers what he believed to be the truth, and claimed that his "generation will certainly not pass away until all these things have happened" (Mark 13:30). They "will not taste death before they see that the kingdom of" Yahweh "has come to power" (Mark 9:1). The disciples, like Paul, did not live to see these events take place. Again, they were wrong.

Right after claiming to have knowledge about the timing of the end of the world, Jesus admits that no one knows when it will happen, not even him. Jesus failed to know because "no one knows" "about that day or hour, not even the angels in heaven, nor the Son, but only the Father" (Mark 13:32). This means that only Yahweh holds that knowledge. Jesus has no idea when the end will take place. He was even aware of his own ignorance, yet he still promised an inaccurate time frame for Yahweh's apocalypse. The Christian demigod knowingly lied. Why would anyone continue to trust his predictions after such an obvious oversight?

Yahweh is the only one who knows the day and the hour of his apocalypse. He tells us in the Bible that it will happen "soon" (Revelation 3:11). "The time is near," Yahweh says (Revelation 1:3). Again and again, he states that his apocalypse will be "coming soon"

(Revelation 22:7). Jesus claimed the end was going to take place during his time on earth. Paul thought he was going to see Jesus in the clouds first hand and most Christians today believe the same thing as Paul. The Bible has managed to convince countless people that Jesus is going to return within their lifetime. Generation after generation, Christians have continued to believe that they will see Jesus coming in the clouds to take them home. Every single one of them has been wrong.

Inevitably, when nothing happens, when people start to notice that Jesus is a no show, Yahweh fortuitously predicted through his prophet Peter, that some would begin to question the validity of "this coming," this end of the world that was "promised" (2 Peter 3:4). They would recall being told that their "ancestors" would live to see the end, yet their "ancestors" would have all "died," and the world would have continued to endure just as it had "since the beginning of creation" (2 Peter 3:4). According to Peter, everyone was wrong about the timing of these events, even Jesus. He indicated that Yahweh "is not slow in keeping his promise, as some understand slowness" (2 Peter 3:9). He believed that the reason it appeared to be taking longer than it should be was due to our misunderstanding of Yahweh's concept of time. Peter asserted that to the Christian deity "a day is like a thousand years, and a thousand years is like a day" (2 Peter 3:8).

This idea, however, could not possibly be applied to every biblical timeline, time frame, or period of time described within the pages of Yahweh's bestseller. Without verification from their mute deity, Christians, using their own thought processes, must choose which stories to apply this Yahwistic concept of time to. If we adopt this idea of one day being equivalent to one thousand years and apply it to some of the other stories within the biblical texts, we would have a world that was created not in days but millennia and a demigod deceased for three thousand years instead of the typically taught three days in the tomb. This idea is not consistent with the rest of the biblical narrative; it does not fit. Peter did not know why the apocalypse had not yet taken place. As an excuse for this delay, Peter changes the timeline for these events by inventing an entirely new concept of time, Yahweh time.

As if abandoning his new schedule change for the apocalypse, Peter, later on, attempts to warn those living in his lifetime of the impending destruction of the world. He wanted them to "look forward to the day" when Yahweh would return to "bring about the destruction of the heavens by fire" (2 Peter 3:12). He claimed that "the day of the" Christian apocalypse "will come like a thief" and that "the heavens will disappear with a roar" and "the earth and everything done in it will be laid bare" (2 Peter 3:10). Why would Peter warn these people about an end he believed would not happen for thousands of years? Peter appears to be confused as to when he thinks the end will come.

Once he feels that an adequate amount of time has passed, Yahweh, the loving deity worshiped by Christians, will launch his final genocide. The Christian apocalypse will begin with "a scroll" that has "writing on both sides and" is "sealed with seven seals" (Revelation 5:1). "No one in heaven or on the earth or under the earth" will be able to "open the scroll or even look inside it" (Revelation 5:3). Not even the all-powerful Christian deity himself. The only one capable of breaking the seven unbreakable seals will be Jesus disguised as "a Lamb, looking as if it had been slain" (Revelation 5:6). He will appear "standing at the center of" Yahweh's eccentric "throne, encircled by" twenty-four "elders" and "four living creatures" who will have six wings and be covered entirely with eyeballs (Revelation 5:6).

Jesus will arrive disguised as a dead lamb with "seven horns and seven eyes" on his head (Revelation 5:7). Once dead lamb Jesus takes "the scroll from the right hand of" Yahweh, "the four living" six-winged eyeball monsters and their companions, the "twenty-four elders," will fall "down before" dead "Lamb" Jesus (Revelation 5:7-8). "Each one" will have "a harp" and "golden bowls full of incense," and they will sing "a new song," praising the one who is "worthy to take the scroll and open its seals" (Revelation 5:8-9). After which, "ten thousand times ten thousand" "angels" "in a loud voice" will sing, "Worthy is the Lamb who was slain, to receive power and

wealth and wisdom and strength and honor and glory and praise"
(Revelation 5:11-12). "Every creature in heaven and on earth and
under the earth and on the sea, and all that is in them" will sing
"praise and honor and glory and power, for ever and ever" to Yahweh
and "the Lamb" (Revelation 5:13). Every animal on the planet will
stop what they are doing and sing a song. The Christian apocalypse
will include singing animals. At the beginning of the Bible, there is
a talking snake that convinces two people to eat magical fruit, and
by the end of the book, earthworms will be singing praises to a demigod dressed in a dead lamb costume.

The flying eyeball monsters will close out the song that every person on the planet will be singing alongside their dogs, with an
"amen," while the twenty-four "elders" fall "down and" worship
Yahweh yet again (Revelation 5:14). Why does he need every living
creature to worship and sing praises to him? Why does he require
these songs to be sung? Why are there singing animals in the Christian apocalypse?

After all life on earth has finished singing their flattering chorus
line, Jesus, still disguised as a deceased "Lamb" with an excessive
number of eyeballs, will open "the first of the seven seals" (Revelation
6:1). This first broken seal will release upon the world "a white
horse" whose rider will hold a "bow, and" be "given a crown" (Revelation 6:2). He will ride "out as a conqueror bent on conquest"
(Revelation 6:2).

When dead "Lamb" Jesus opens up "the second seal," a "fiery
red" "horse" will come out and be "given power to take peace from
the earth," causing "people" to "kill each other" (Revelation 6:3-4).
With the "third seal...a black horse" will come out whose "rider"
will be "holding a pair of scales in his hand" (Revelation 6:5). "The
fourth seal" will bring "a pale horse" whose "rider" will be "named
Death, and Hades" will be "following close behind him" (Revelation
6:7-8). He will be "given power over a fourth of the earth to kill by
sword, famine and plague, and by the wild beasts of the earth" (Revelation 6:8). According to the Christian holy texts, during the end of

the world, people riding horses will come out of a scroll and cause death and destruction upon the earth.

When the "fifth seal" is broken, a group of "souls" that have died for their beliefs will ask Yahweh "in a loud voice, how long" it would be until he judges "the inhabitants of the earth," avenging their deaths (Revelation 6:9-10). When Yahweh hears what these souls are asking, he thanks them for their patience, gives them "a white robe," and tells them to "wait" some more. (Revelation 6:11). This particular event seems like such a waste of a seal. The entire seal gets used up by a group of impatient souls who will interrupt Yahweh's finale only to complain about how long it is taking. The Bible says that all it will take to calm these restless souls and their thirst for vengeance is a white robe. Do these robes have some sort of relaxation spell on them? Or does the Christian deity not provide his servants with robes in heaven? The Bible continues to leave us so many unanswered questions.

Once dead lamb Jesus opens up "the sixth seal" there will be "a great earthquake, the sun" will turn "black like sackcloth made of goat hair, the whole moon" will become "blood red and the stars" will fall "to the earth" (Revelation 6:12-13). After his impractical star falling event, the Christian deity will take away the sky by rolling it up "like a scroll" (Revelation 6:14). He will take "every mountain and island" and have them "removed from its place" (Revelation 6:14). Upon seeing this happen, humans will run and hide "in caves and among the rocks of the mountains" that were previously removed (Revelation 6:15).

Eventually, dead lamb Jesus will break "the seventh" and final "seal" (Revelation 8:1). When he does, there will be "silence in heaven for about half an hour" (Revelation 8:1). Yahweh neglects to specify if this half-hour of silence will be in Yahweh years or if it will take place in a regular time frame—the Bible does not say. During this heavenly moment of silence, "seven angels" will be silently "given" "seven trumpets" with which to rain down terror upon the earth (Revelation 8:2).

After dead lamb Jesus has broken all of the seals, the angels will blow their magical trumpets. With the "trumpet" blast from "the first angel...hail and fire mixed with blood" will be "hurled down upon the earth," causing "a third of the earth" to be "burned up" (Revelation 8:7). "The second angel" will blow his horn "and something like a huge mountain, all ablaze," will be "thrown into the sea," killing off "a third of the living creatures" and destroying "a third of the ships" on the planet (Revelation 8:8-9). With the sound of the "third...trumpet...a great star, blazing like a torch" will fall "from the sky" onto "a third of the rivers and...springs of water" (Revelation 8:10). "The waters" will become "bitter" causing "many people" to die (Revelation 8:11). Yahweh is going to name his impossible falling star "Wormwood" (Revelation 8:11). After the "fourth...trumpet" blast, "a third of the sun...a third of the moon, and a third of the stars," will all be "struck" and "turned dark" (Revelation 8:12).

When there are only three angels with three trumpets left to sound, "an eagle" will fly around the world and "call out in a loud voice: 'Woe! 'Woe! 'Woe...because of the trumpet blasts about to be sounded by the other three angels" (Revelation 8:13). Yahweh needed his apocalypse to include a talking eagle that flies around the world, yelling "Woe!" Why are there so many talking animals in the Christian holy book? People know that animals cannot talk, yet they put their trust in a book that says not only can they talk, but they can sing as well.

"The fifth angel" will blow his horn and Yahweh's star, Wormwood, will get a "key to the shaft of the Abyss" (Revelation 9:1). Once the key has been used, "the Abyss" will open, smoke will rise up, and what is left of the "sun and sky" will be "darkened by the smoke" (Revelation 9:2). "Out of the smoke" will come "locusts" with tails that sting like "scorpions" (Revelation 9:3). They will come "down on the earth" and sting anyone who does "not have the seal of" Yahweh "on their foreheads" (Revelation 9:3-4). Those unlucky enough to be stung by one of these creatures will not die from the venom it produces. Yahweh created a poison designed to "torture" people "for five months" (Revelation 9:5). Again, it is unclear if this five-month duration is using Peter's Yahwistic concept of time or not, it does not say.

During the months or years of torture that accompanies being stung by these impossible creatures, "people will seek death but will not find it; they will long to die, but death will elude them" (Revelation 9:6). Yahweh's scorpion locusts will have "something like crowns of gold" on their heads, "and their faces" will resemble "human faces" (Revelation 9:7). They will have "hair…like women's hair, and their teeth" will be "like lions' teeth" (Revelation 9:8). Yahweh will instruct his modified monsters "not to harm the grass of the earth or any plant or tree" (Revelation 9:4). They are under strict orders to only attack those who do not have Yahweh's seal of approval on their foreheads. Why are these strange creatures needed at all? Why would a loving being create and deploy monsters to terrorize and cause harm to people?

When the "trumpet" from "the sixth angel" is "sounded," four other "angels who had been kept ready for this very hour and day and month and year," will be released (Revelation 9:13-15). These angels will be riding horse-like creatures with heads that resemble "the heads of lions" and "tails" that are "like snakes," capable of inflicting "injury" (Revelation 9:17-19). These nightmare creatures will have the ability to emit "fire, smoke, and sulfur" from "out of their mouths" (Revelation 9:18). These "four" special "angels" will "kill a third of mankind" using their weaponized equine (Revelation 9:15).

When "the seventh" and final "angel" sounds "his trumpet," Yahweh will open the door to his "temple in heaven," causing "flashes of lightning, rumblings, peals of thunder, an earthquake," just one, "and a severe hail storm" in the process (Revelation 11:15-19). With this concluding trumpet sound, Yahweh will proceed to the final phase of his musical apocalypse.

The Christian deity will send out "seven angels" who will carry with them "the seven last plagues" (Revelation 15:1). These angels will be "dressed in clean, shining linen" with "golden sashes around their chests" (Revelation 15:6). They will be holding "seven golden bowls" that will be "filled with the wrath of" Yahweh (Revelation 15:7). These will be the last plagues he inflicts upon the world "because with them," the "wrath" of the Christian deity will be "completed" (Revelation 15:1).

Yahweh will need these seven angels to "pour out the seven bowls" containing his "wrath" onto "the earth" one at a time (Revelation 16:1). "The first angel" will pour "out his bowl" of Yahweh anger onto "the land," causing people to break out with painful, "ugly, festering sores" all over their bodies (Revelation 16:2). "The second angel" will pour "out his bowl" of wrath into "the sea," turning it to "blood, like that of a dead man," killing "every living thing in" it (Revelation 16:3). The all-powerful Christian deity is capable of eradicating sea life any way he pleases. He could snap his fingers and stop their hearts or he could make them vanish off the face of the earth. In the end, he chose the option he thought was best. Drown them in wrathful blood water. This is what pleases Yahweh. This is his show.

"The third angel" will pour "out his bowl" of Yahweh wrath "on the rivers and springs of water, and they" too will become "blood" (Revelation 16:4). Yahweh believes that those who will have survived his apocalypse thus far "deserve" to spend their last days having nothing but "blood to drink" (Revelation 16:6). "The fourth angel" is going to pour "out his bowl on the sun," giving it the "power to scorch people with fire" (Revelation 16:8). Yahweh wants them to suffer because they refuse "to repent and glorify him" (Revelation 16:9). Apologize and worship the loving Christian deity, or he will burn you with the sun.

"The fifth angel" will pour "out his bowl on the throne of the beast," plunging it "into darkness" (Revelation 16:10). "The sixth angel" will pour "out his" golden "bowl on the great river Euphrates" causing it to dry up (Revelation 16:12). "The seventh" and final "bowl" of Yahweh wrath will be "poured out...into the air," and Yahweh will cry out in "a loud voice...'It is done,'" signifying the end of the wrathful "bowl" pouring portion of his apocalypse (Revelation 16:17).

"Then there" will come "flashes of lightning, rumblings, peals of thunder" and another earthquake (Revelation 16:18). This time the "earthquake" will be so big that "no" other "earthquake like it has ever occurred since mankind has been on earth" (Revelation 16:18). Yahweh will again remove "every island" and topple all "the mountains" (Revelation 16:20). He will cause "hailstones, each weighing about a hundred pounds" to fall down "on people" (Revelation 16:21).

Once the Christian deity has finished his pointlessly theatrical rampage, he is going to open up "the book of life" and judge "each person...according to what they had done" (Revelation 20:12-13). He is going to find out if you have been naughty or nice. His magic book knows all your deep dark secrets. The book of life will help Yahweh decide whether he should send you to his "city of pure gold" (Revelation 21:18) or "into the lake of fire" for all eternity (Revelation 20:15). The all-knowing Christian deity will rely on a book and not his own knowledge. He is unable to remember everything about every person's life and requires a book to keep it all in.

Through his own breathed out words, the Christian deity describes his violent intentions to eradicate every creature living on the planet. Christians will often enthusiastically refer to the end of the world as the tribulation, the rapture, or the end times. Most believe that their "citizenship is in heaven" (Philippians 3:20), and that their demigod in sandals will be arriving soon "in clouds with great power and glory" to take them home (Mark 13:26). Most Christians cannot contain their joy and excitement as they anxiously await the day when their deity comes back to kill everyone and set fire to the earth.

Yahweh has chosen to torture, burn, and slaughter everyone that will not worship him, everyone that does not love him as the Christians do. You will worship and love the angry Christian deity, or he will force you to endure his dramatic end of days and then burn you for all eternity. Love me or suffer, worship at my feet, or I will throw you into a lake of fire. These are not the commands of a being that deserves to be glorified and praised. The Christian deity should be mocked and treated with contempt for his needlessly eccentric demands and indifference toward living beings. I will never understand why anyone would want to worship such a monster.

Outro

Most Christians start with the concept that Yahweh is the good guy in the story. This is why when Yahweh kills a bunch of kids the believer has to somehow rationalize the monstrous actions of their loving, just deity. The decisions made by Yahweh in the Bible go against our natural sensibilities, our empathetic radar. Most of us are able to understand the difference between what is absolutely abhorrent and cruel and what is pleasurable and agreeable. Unfortunately, most Christians assume before they investigate.

When you start with a predetermined outcome, your research and findings become an attempt to fit the premise you started with. No matter the amount of twisting and special pleading it takes, Christians will make sure that what they find is going to line up with their beliefs.

If your grandma told you about that one time she decided to drown a bunch of kids because they wouldn't listen to her, would you still find her loving? If you found out that she built a torture chamber where she would send those who don't love her, would you find her actions just and fair? Of course not. So why does Yahweh continue to get a pass for all of the pointless death, destruction, and pain he causes throughout his bestseller?

Despite the fact, many Christians have not read beyond the shiny happy Jesus portions of the Bible their pastor slings from the pulpit every Sunday, they will argue till their last breath that their Bible is a good book full of amazing stories and helpful insights. When introduced to the child-killing, misogynistic deity described by the

Bible, the Christian mind will either reject its validity or accept it and find an excuse for the deplorable actions of their best friend. When they accept his role in the slaughter of countless people, the Christian will claim that something good will come from the tragedy. They assume there is some sort of silver lining to every appalling thing he does.

No matter how many inhumane stories and commands the Bible contains, no matter what atrocities Yahweh commits, Christians will stand by their deity and their holy book. They feel they have an obligation, a duty to stand up for their defenseless invisible friend and his barbaric ideas. Their pride is connected to their belief in Yahweh. Point out his flaws, and the Christian becomes defensive. Some will even turn to apologetics to find the excuses they need to continue in their belief.

When Christians try to prove the realness of their deity, all their claims boil down to a feeling or a personal experience. The Christian-Yahweh connection is nothing more than a feeling and a hope. Christianity is built on both. Making it fragile and easily discredited. My journey through the theistic world has led me to the realization that the Christian belief is fragile. Remarkably, this is a fact in which I think most of them are aware. They have no hard evidence for their invisible, mute deity. They all fail to present any credible arguments or rational concepts to the conversation. They have no good reason for their beliefs. Yahweh refuses to come down from his cloud and say hello. It would make things a lot easier for Christians if he did. Yet, Yahweh is a no show. Without proof, without hard evidence of Yahweh's existence, Christians have to pretend he is there using faith. Christians use their faith to fill the gaps in both common sense and confirmation. Faith, for most Christians, is a mindset of just believe it, and it will be true. Believe that you have been saved by invisible magical blood, then you will be saved. It's a ridiculous concept.

According to the Bible, Christians can use this faith to perform extraordinary feats that defy reality. The Christian demigod told his followers that with just a wee bit of "faith," anyone can "say to" a "mountain, 'Move from here to there,' and it will move" (Matthew

17:20). "Nothing will be impossible for" those with enough faith (Matthew 17:20). In the book of Luke, Jesus claims that with the power of "faith," one can "say to" a "tree, 'Be uprooted and planted in the sea,' and it will obey" (Luke 17:6). No Christian has been able to demonstrate this ability.

But wait there is more. According to the Bible, faith can be used to give people their "sight" back (Mark 10:52). Got a demon-possessed daughter? Apply a little "faith," and she will be "healed at that moment" (Matthew 15:28). The book of Ephesians says "faith" can be used as a "shield" to "extinguish all the flaming arrows of the evil one" (Ephesians 6:16). And Paul wants us all to believe that Christians "live by faith, not by sight" (2 Corinthians 5:7).

The Bible says Christians can use these Yahweh-ordained magic powers to affect the real world. Attending one of these faith healing churches is equivalent to LARPing (live action role playing), but for Christians. They will dramatically attempt to pray away tumors, demons, tornadoes, or even global pandemics. All without any miraculous end. Natural cause and natural disasters play out as if no higher being or magical person had any effect on its relentless, methodical course toward death and destruction. Without the wishful thinking of Christians, nothing changes.

When Christians are unable to use their faith powers as the Bible says they should be able to, they will either blame themselves for not having the correct amount of faith or assert the inconceivable notion of moving the unmovable as mere hyperbole. Reality is not on their side. Christians must retreat into the fanciful. They must resort to a world of make-believe.

I am empathetic to those ensnared in the lies and empty promises brought by religion. I have been there. I used to think that all of my successes were made possible by Yahweh. He alone was allowing me to complete projects or make it through a difficult time. What took me years to come to terms with was that I did it all without his help. There was no invisible man in the sky magically assisting me. People are stronger and more resilient than they give themselves credit for. There is no need to thank a deified child killer. Give yourself a giant pat on the back for your accomplishments, because Jesus didn't even bother to show up.

There is a lot I do not understand or fully comprehend. And I'm ok with that. I accept my ignorance about a great many things, and I work toward a better understanding. That is how I grow as a person. This is how I better myself.

Yahweh, on the other hand, claims to be all-knowing in 1 John 3:20. Yet throughout the Bible, we find blatant examples of the opposite. In Leviticus 15:19-31 Yahweh fails to know what a woman's monthly cycle is. The all-knowing Christian deity thinks period blood contains a highly contagious form of the cooties that can easily be spread throughout an entire town if precautions are not taken.

According to Genesis 11:5, the Christian deity did not know what was going on in the city of Sodom. He needed to go down and take a look to see if what he had heard was true. In the book of Job, Yahweh failed to know where his arch-nemesis had been. After which he was unable to realize in time that the Devil had convinced him to kill a bunch innocent people. (Job 2:3). In Genesis 22, the all-knowing Christian deity failed to know how dedicated to the cause his friend Abraham was. Yahweh decided the best way for his friend to prove his loyalty was for him to murder his son. Abraham obliged and almost slaughtered his kid as a sacrifice to his loving deity.

One of the most obvious things Yahweh failed to realize was that his promotion and condoning of slavery was wrong. In the New Testament, we find that Yahweh commands "slaves" to "obey" their "masters with respect and fear" (Ephesians 6:5). He finds these monsters to be deserving of the same level of honor shown to the Christian demigod himself. The Christian deity clearly has no issue with owning people as property. These are not the demands of a compassionate all-knowing being.

When a Christian is unable to understand why their loving deity would condone such a despicable act, most do not refute or question him. Instead, they come up with excuses for these inhumane demands from their perfect deity. They have to make the really bad stuff sound better and less harsh in some way, they have to turn their deity's disgusting policies and commands into something palatable.

These kinds of ideas need to be challenged and confronted. Not shrugged off, watered down, or brushed under the rug. These issues need to be brought into the light and exposed for the disgusting ideas they are. Christians worship a being that not only advocates for the enslavement of human beings, he is also a documented child killer. Why would anyone want to worship such a monster?

That's all the book there is for you today, thanks for reading.

About the Author

Michael Wiseman is a former Christian, and the host of "The Bible Says What!?" the podcast. This atheist vs. Christian style show captures Michael's one on one conversations with religious leaders from across the globe.

Michael was born and raised in a strict Christian home, where belief was not a choice but a requirement. Using the fear of eternal hellfire, he was indoctrinated into the evangelical, holy-roller flavor of Christianity. Baptized and teaching Sunday School, Michael was hard-core for Jesus. As he grew older, so did his doubts. Sitting down and reading the Bible led him to question his beliefs and doubt the validity of his fears.

Now an outspoken atheist, Michael uses his knowledge of the Bible to challenge the beliefs of the faithful. Using their own holy book, he encourages believers to look into their strongly held beliefs. He spreads his unique slice of blasphemy and firebrand atheism from his make-shift recording studio in Las Vegas NV, where he lives with his wife and two boys.

www.ingramcontent.com/pod-product-compliance
Lightning Source LLC
Chambersburg PA
CBHW021930040426

42448CB00008B/997